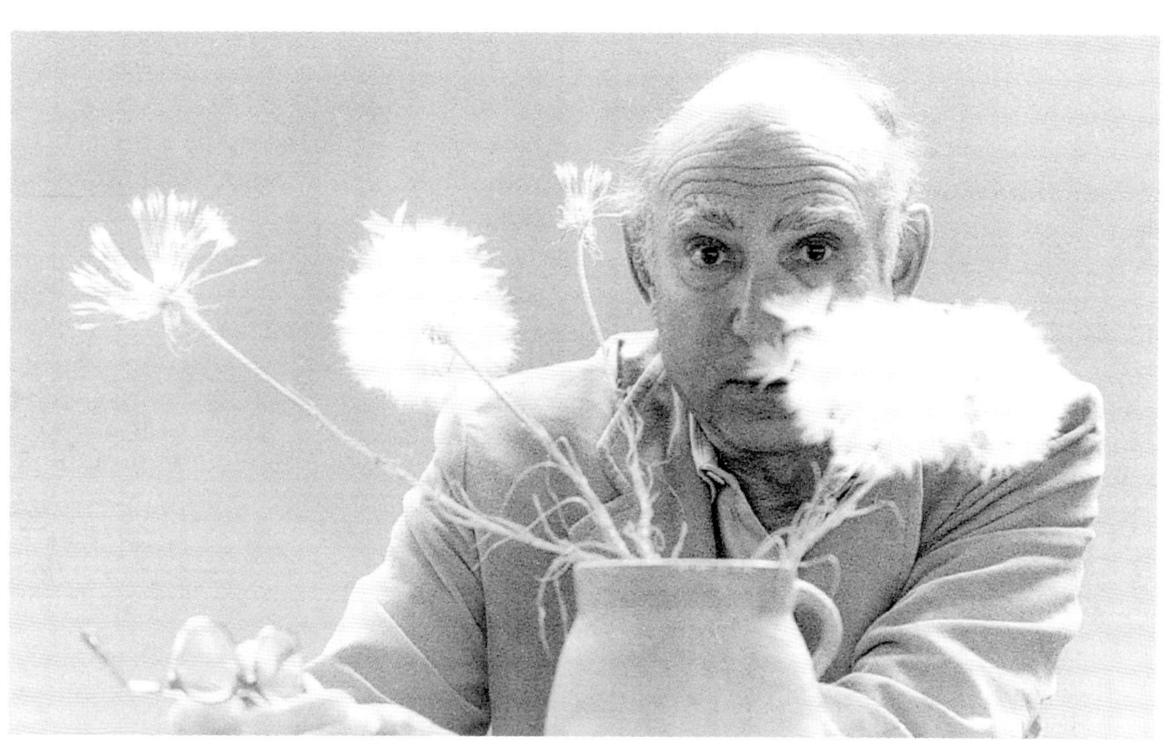

Peter Takal on paper

Townsend Wolfe

Peter Takal on paper

Townsend Wolfe

June 2 – July 30, 2000

SPONSORED BY

Letty and Hall McAdams

Virginia and Ted Bailey

Helen Porter and James T. Dyke

Sandy and A. Dan Phillips

SUPPORTED IN PART BY GRANTS FROM

The Judith Rothschild Foundation

The Henry Luce Foundation, Inc.

Arkansas Arts Center
Donald W. Reynolds Drawing & Research Center

Published by
Arkansas Museum of Art
Donald W. Reynolds Drawing & Research Center

Arkansas Arts Center

MacArthur Park
501 East 9th Street
Little Rock, Arkansas 72202
501-372-4000 / fax: 501-375-8053
P.O. Box 2137, 72203

DIRECTOR AND CHIEF CURATOR:
Townsend Wolfe

CURATOR OF ART:
Brian Young

REGISTRAR:
Thom Hall

PREPARATOR:
Keith Melton

CURATORIAL ASSISTANT:
Anne Gochenour

ISBN 1-884240-22-4

ENGRAVING:
Magna IV IGI

PHOTOGRAPHY:
Cindy Momchilov
Pla Narbona, *Peter Takal,* circa 1969, p. 3

COVER:
Man Wearing Hat, 1979, p. 85

Unless otherwise noted, all works are the promised gift of the Takal estate.

Supported in part by the Arkansas Arts Council

Note: All dimensions are in inches. Height precedes width.

Peter Takal

Perhaps not since Jean-Auguste-Dominique Ingres (1780-1867) has there been an artist who was so focused on drawing as a means of expression as Peter Takal (1905-1995). Both artists were dedicated to the ultimate use of line to clarify and state their observations and inner spirit. Of course, Picasso and Matisse drew incessantly, but not with the finite conviction of Takal to the drawing medium. George Wildenstein wrote in his book, *Ingres,* 1956, "so it is by drawing that Ingres regains contact with his God." I would say the same about Peter Takal—a master drawer who never considered the medium a means to an end. For Takal, drawing was the highest form of art.

With this said, you can imagine my response when I received a telephone call from Jean Takal (Mrs. Peter Takal) of Geneva, Switzerland, on August 5, 1996. Jean had learned about the Arkansas Arts Center's focus and commitment to the medium of drawing from Sylvan Cole, a New York art dealer and long-time admirer of Takal. In October 1996, Jean, her son, Pierre Takal, and I met in New York to discuss Peter's work and the Arts Center's commitment to drawing. At this time, the idea of the Center becoming a possible home for Peter's drawings began to take shape. In November 1997, I flew to Geneva and reviewed 5,000 drawings and sketchbooks. Through all the various sheets, I saw a life devoted to drawing unfold before me. In September 1998, Jean, Pierre, and I spoke concretely about the Arkansas Arts Center creating a definitive repository collection as well as a study and archival research center on Takal. In November of 1999, I again visited Geneva, and selected approximately 2,000 drawings and sketchbooks to form the core collection.

This exhibition of seventy-two drawings is the first of many to come. One might wonder if these seventy-two sheets represent the best of the 2,000. The answer is—there is no best. We have the 2,000 best! However, the selected seventy-two reflect the life and range of Peter Takal. These works introduce Peter Takal, an artist who is a master drawer. As you will see, it is the touch of the artist on paper with ink, crayon, pencil, charcoal, and watercolor that brings the surface of the sheet to life. Like Ingres, Takal deals with all subjects with equal attentiveness, conscientiousness, and honesty. His grace of line and vibrant flow create intoxicating poetry.

At times, his touch is gentle and sensual, imparting a mysterious quality to the image. This touch, ranging in dates and subject matter, is apparent in the following works: *Reclining Woman,* Paris, 1931, p. 25, *Reclining Woman,* Paris, 1932, p. 27, *Creek in Forest,* Nevada, 1956, p. 54, *Grasses in Bottle,* Saylorsburg, Pennsylvania, 1962, p. 63, *Torso,* Geneva, 1975, p. 80, and *Field,* Geneva, 1991, p. 91.

In contrast, a more calligraphic line and touch creating a rhythm energizing the image is found in these pen and ink works: *Dish with Pears,* Saylorsburg, 1945, p. 42, *Flowering Vine and Clouds,* Mexico, 1959, p. 56, *Oranges,* Spain, 1961, p. 61, *Back of a Woman's Head,* Saylorsburg, 1963, p. 64, *Clouds,* Saylorsburg, 1966, p. 70, and *Phoenix,* Geneva, 1975, p. 79. These pieces employ more direct, contained, and descriptive lines. This effect is equally sensual and seductive. The use of this bolder touch also appears throughout Takal's career as the mood and need for additional clarity emerges. The bolder line is freer in *Dandy,* New York, 1945, p. 41, *Nude with Parasol,* 1955, p. 51, and *Road and Woods,* Saylorsburg, 1957, p. 55. These contrast with the more straightforward treatment of natural objects found in *Wood Stove and Chair,* Saylorsburg, 1955, p. 50, *Tree Bark,* Mexico, 1959, p. 58, and *Tree,* Saylorsburg, 1965, p. 69.

Through constant observation and imagination, Takal's expressive hand creates dreamlike sheets which possess a haunting surreal quality. Examples include *Tunnel,* New York, 1956, p. 52, *View Through Curtains,* Mexico, 1959, p. 57, *Splintered Log,* Yaddo, New York, 1961, p. 60, *Fish Heads,* Maine, 1967, p. 74, *Blotter Gossip,* Geneva, 1973, p. 77, and the two lustrous Geneva landscapes—*Slope,* 1971, p. 76, and *Landscape,* 1978, p. 84. Takal was much like Picasso in spirit, confidence, and drive to work and make art. His style was his own, what others did had no bearing on him. His touch is his spirit and his style. The drawings of people and faces, covering over sixty years, help guide us in the understanding of both the man and the artist.

The serious look, conveyed with sparse, contour lines in *Woman in Chair,* Paris, 1930, p. 21, contrasts with textured, detailed marks in *Sisters,* Paris, 1931, p. 23. The relaxed *Woman Sleeping,* Paris, 1933, p. 29, fills the page with a deliberate and peaceful line of ink implying a different mood than the piercing glare of the *Little Boy at a Table,* Morocco, 1937, p. 34. A vague suggestion of form, character, and temperament infuse grace into *Subway Rider,* New York, 1954, p. 47, *Woman at Roof Edge,* New York, 1956, p. 53, and *Man Wearing Hat,* Saylorsburg, 1979, p. 85. And finally, *Face,* Geneva, 1989, p. 89, and *Face with Half-closed Eye,* Geneva, 1992, p. 92, capture the emotional directness and humanity found in all of his drawings.

The exhibition and catalogue are made possible with the good work and help of the Arts Center staff, particularly Thom Hall, Registrar; Brian Young, Curator of Art; Anne Gochenour, Curatorial Assistant; Keith Melton, Preparator. I am grateful to our sponsors Letty and Hall McAdams, Virginia and Ted Bailey, Helen Porter and James T. Dyke, Sandy and A. Dan Phillips and to the Henry Luce Foundation and the Judith Rothschild Foundation for encouragement and support.

I am thankful to Jean Takal and Pierre Takal for introducing me to this important and glorious body of work. I am mindful and appreciative of the time and work they spent in organizing the seven decades for me to review. Most of all I want them to know that the life and work of Peter Takal honors the Arkansas Arts Center collection with its presence.

The Art of Peter Takal is made of

Lines that are the vision of the maker

Lines that sing with soul

Lines that see what has never been

Lines that give thoughts a heart

Lines that contain what is uncontainable

Lines that caress with the search

Lines that reveal our humanity

Lines that touch our very being

Lines that reflect what is felt

Lines that breath life in every sheet

Lines that make the surreal a reality

Lines that give hope to the spirit

Lines that are the magic we call art.

Townsend Wolfe
Director and Chief Curator
Arkansas Arts Center
May, 2000

of a picture, confined within its square, expands without limits beyond its physical dimensions through the stimulant of our imagination (imagination is the inner vision). A picture may often promote a sensation of rhythm or sound which gives, beyond the first visual contact, other and deeper sensorial dimensions.

Thus, our inner senses are not restricted to the range of our outer receptive organs. The inner senses give amplitude to the sensations received by the eye, the ear, the nose, and the touch. The inner senses communicate freely within us; it is their activity that deepens the outer sensations.

It does not seem to me farfetched to compare a picture with a person whose visible and invisible qualities release in us certain reactions. There are those whose eye-appeal may wear off fast. The spectacular or sensational with which we have been infatuated, may soon leave us with an embarrassing feeling of emptiness. On the other hand, there are those whose presence gives us a precious feeling of well-being, of moral comfort. These people, and these pictures, will be our preferred ones: they will continue to give us enduring enjoyment.

It is not easy for me to write about my own work. Whatever I now attempt to say cannot be more than an approximate and inadequate explanation of the language of lines and forms. I resist, furthermore, the fallacy of attempting to intellectualize an activity which has as its tools my senses and nerves only. While I work, my brain rests, comfortably inactive. Since I am almost always working, I can easily dispense with the brain which is probably the organ I would miss the least.

This does not mean that I don't think. But, my thoughts are not in technological, philosophical or scientific terms. My thoughts are in terms of heavy, light, pointed, blunt, blurred, round, square, limpid, opaque, hard, soft, steady, shifting, far, near, vast, narrow, condensed, misty, and red, blue, yellow, and white, and white, and again white, black, and brown, and so forth.

The horizontal, vertical, and diagonal lines, and the space between them which resounds with their striving, parallel or conflicting directions, represent an interplay of tensions which is full of meaning to me. There is no end to the infinite variety in the universe of lines and forms. They are in a landscape as well as in a twig, in a wave, in a cloud, or in a grasshopper. The confluence of the spectacle of forms, lines, and space with my mood, determines the particular inspiration for the drawing. It may be light and gay, or brooding and tender, or aggressive, witty, dramatic, stenographic, or detailed.

How I apply my observations is conditioned by an inner compulsion, which is also called emotion. This propelling force will determine the composition and the degree of graphic energy with which the drawing is produced.

We cannot find out intellectually why we sympathize with a person. It just happens that we feel good in his or her presence, without questioning. I believe that this feeling alone should make the viewer aware of his sympathy or his dislike for a picture. It is my ambition, however, to engage the viewer before my work in a kind of brainless thinking, in terms of the fictitious sensorial dictionary from which I just quoted a few terms. The viewer will then experience his reactions and will become aware of the meaning in the ink. It would, indeed, be a regrettable misunderstanding and an abuse of the viewer by me if he restricted his view of the pictures to anecdotal contents, in the belief that this was my intention, identifying them as trees, buildings, landscapes, clouds, nudes, and so forth. I am not interested, nor do I want to interest the viewer in the botanical reality of a tree, for instance, the architectural soundness of a building, the anatomical truth of a nude, or in the weather forecast from a drawing of clouds. What motivated me to make these drawings was the particular hour in which these subjects revealed to me their particular face, and prompted me to work in this particular way. The different media and dynamics, the different works dealing with the same subject matter, could not have been done in such variety if my concern had been the rational description of the specific subjects. The dramatic, the tragic, or the lyric aspect of a tree, a cloud, or a so-called "inanimate" object may provoke emotions which are expressed by their graphic equivalent, with a corresponding charge of heroism, pity, humor, scorn, hope, fear, exasperation, tenderness, or exuberance. These various tensions in the work of art may release in the viewer a deeper experience of these emotions than would be permitted by the literal reportage of a sinking boat, or the portrait of death, or languishing ladies in a harem. If an artist intends to capture the attention of the viewer with the literal display of social, political, or moral themes alone, he attempts to arouse the viewer's interest through the exploitation of values extraneous to art.

Why then do I choose the representational form? Well, as an artist, I was born in Paris where, as you know, the "joie de vivre" is paramount. This joy is by no means confined to the "Bal Tabarin," the "Moulin Rouge," or the "Folies Bergères." It is perhaps because of this early love for the visible, the tangible, form that I don't feel the need to destroy it in order to reach the sublime, the marvel and the mystery, the poetic truth in it.

While working, I experience the line or the shape of an object isolated, or in relation to its surroundings. The more I am capable of disregarding, of forgetting, the functional or conventionally assigned properties of the object, the more I feel I succeed in my work. Conventional knowledge of the subject demands the observance of moral or practical standards which would corrupt the consideration of values which alone are valid for my work. Maybe one of the factors which keeps Art ageless is that it is essentially unaffected and unlimited by moral or physical laws and their shifting values.

Musical scores are provided with directions for the mood, the tempo, the meter, and dynamics in which they should be performed. The notation gives the notes values and difference in pitch. Accidentals, fermatas, and rests guide the work, with the help of this chart, through the ocean of music. In a way, a picture is a score that guides the eye through the maze of optical sensations. The fullest meaning of these sensations is not visible in the lines of my work; it is perceptible between the lines, in the way poetry reveals itself between the lines. In any form of Art, the fuller meaning unintelligible to rational thinking reveals itself through our inner senses. It is art which transports us beyond its subject matter to the creative awareness and enjoyment of our emotional capacity.

Some of my graphic work grew in a little valley near Saylorsburg in Pennsylvania, which is inhabited by trees, fields, stones, and birds and their spirits. A long winding narrow dirt road, flanked by fence rows and nut trees, leads towards the West straight into the sky; towards the East, it climbs up to dark woods and is swallowed by them.

This valley is a bowl of goodness that grows four beautiful seasons each year. There I harvest impulses which become lines, forms: pictures. The sky is the big space over my valley into which the trees grow in wintertime, their branches taking root there. There they draw dreams into their sleep. What else does the sky mean to me but that it permits the clouds to appear? In the vastness of nothingness, the clouds sound their whitest of white, sulfur and fire, lead, alabaster, jade, and silver which resound deep in the dome without ceiling. Shadows don't cling to the soft slopes of my valley and the shadows of clouds melt fast there.

The work in the city received different impulses.

The city spells danger, unrest. Man is exposed to Man and to his city-scape. There the heart uses its brain.

In Maine, I became for the first time aware that the sea really *exists.* Before this time the sea was for me more of an element, like air. But I found it playing wild games like an animal, with Sun, Fog, Wind, and Rain. The pulsations of the tides, the painful, oppressing awareness of the last wave, revealing the edge, the limitation of the Sea, the incessant rhythm of give and take, released impulses in my work of which I have been unaware.

Peter Takal

On December 16, 1958, Takal delivered the lecture *Between the Lines* at the Cleveland Museum of Art. In 1961, this lecture was reprinted in *Artist's Proof* published by the Pratt Graphic Art Center.

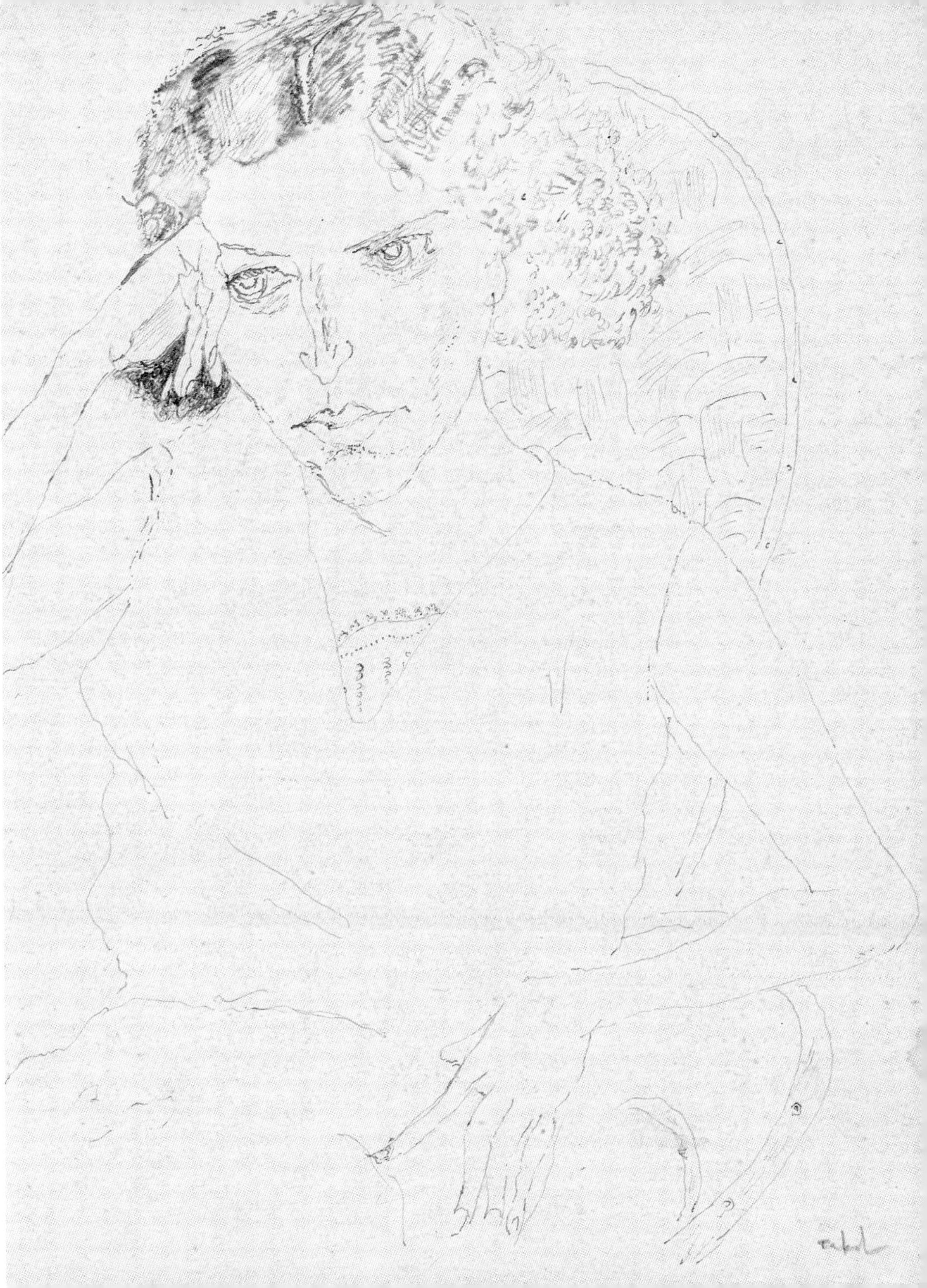

Woman in Chair
Paris, 1930
pen and india ink with blue ink accents on paper
6 1/2 x 5 1/4 inches

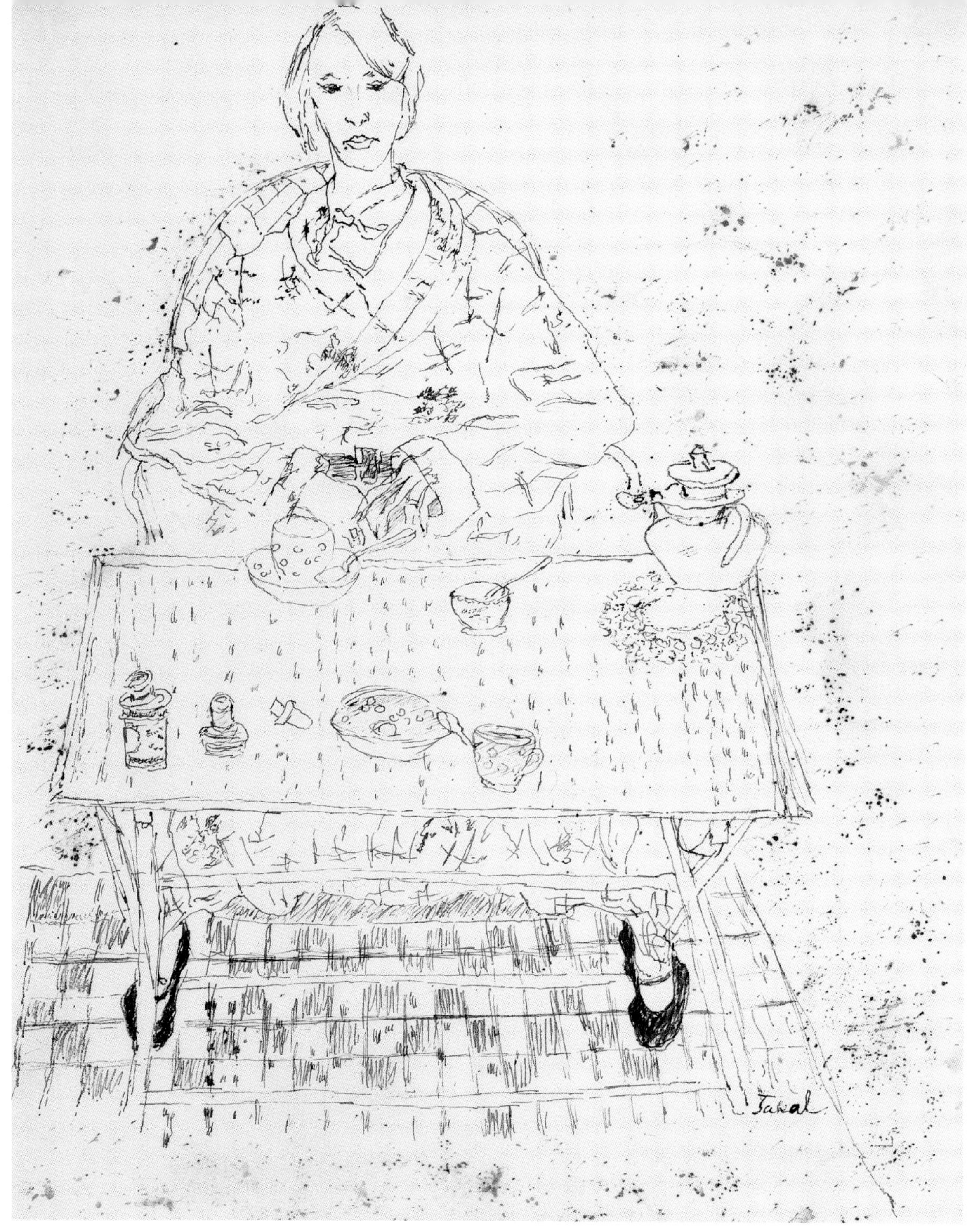

Woman Taking Tea
Paris, 1930
pen and india ink on transparent paper
8 5/8 x 5 3/4 inches

Sisters
Paris, 1931
pen and india ink with blue and brown accents on thin, orange paper
5 3/8 x 7 5/8 inches

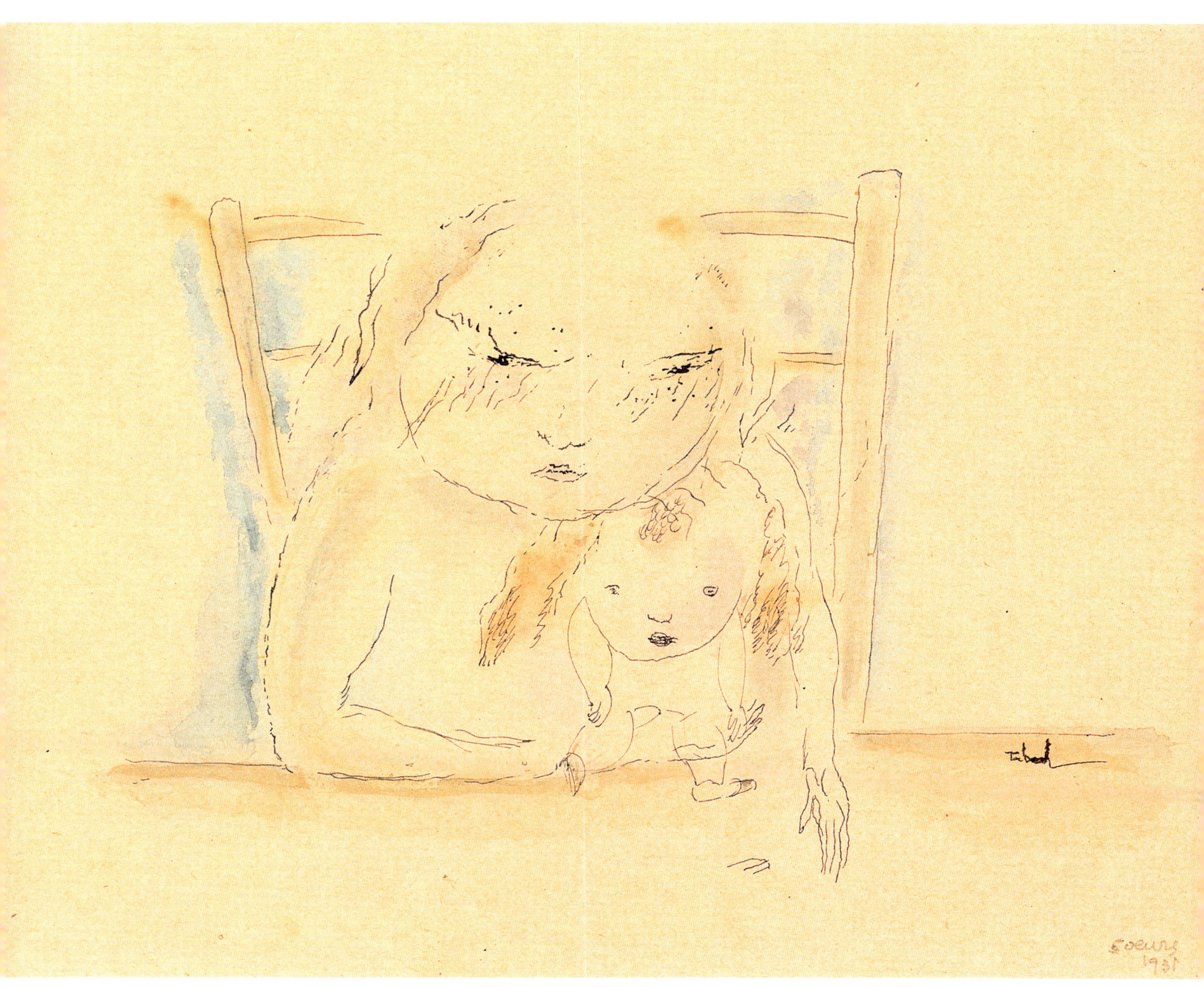

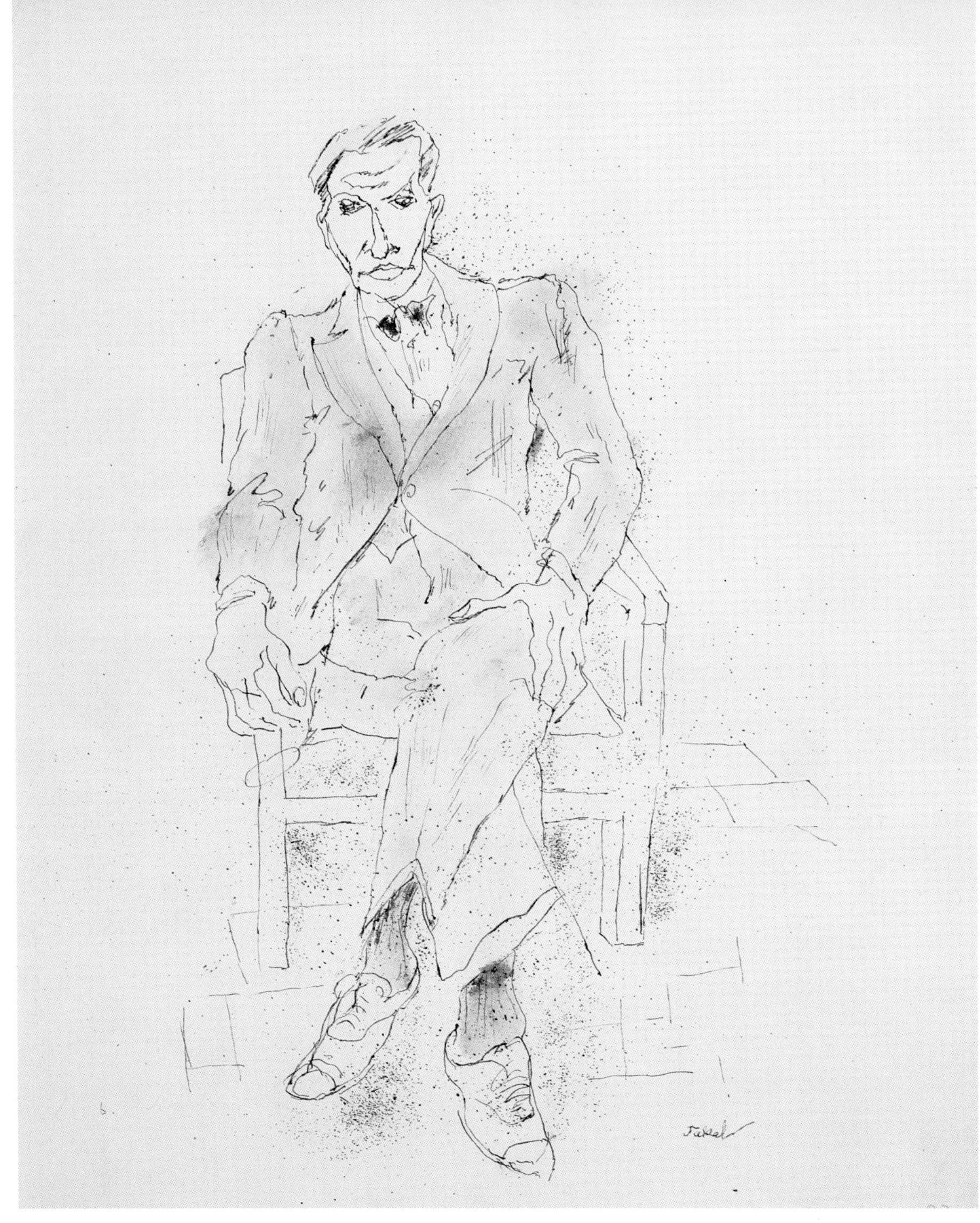

Man with Bowtie
Paris (?), 1931
pen and india ink with brown wash on paper
12 3/8 x 9 5/8 inches

24

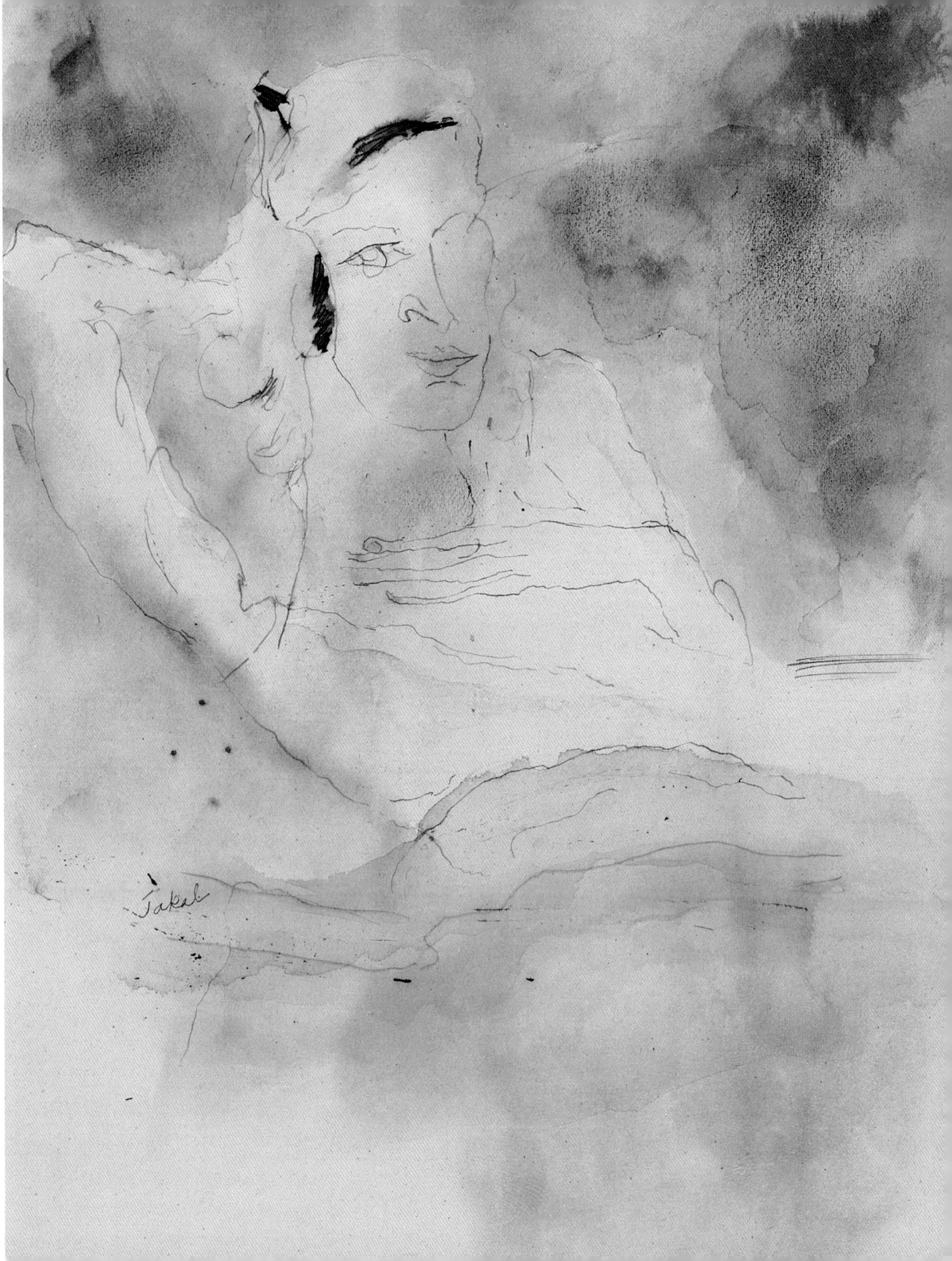

Reclining Woman
Paris, 1931
pen and india ink, watercolor on paper
7 5/8 x 6 inches

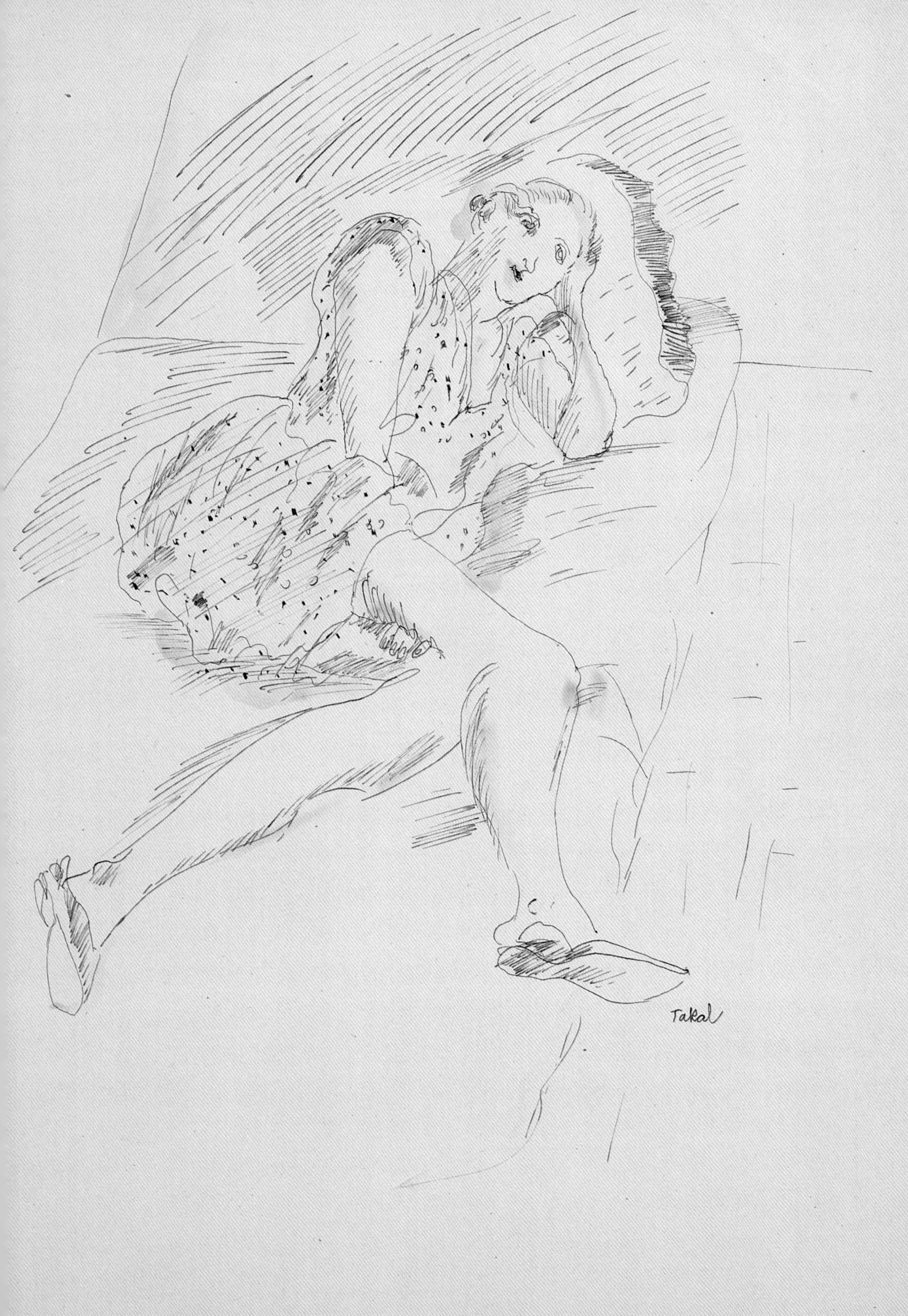

Reclining Woman with Head on Hand
Paris, 1932
pen and india ink with blue, red, and brown accents on paper
18 3/8 x 12 1/2 inches

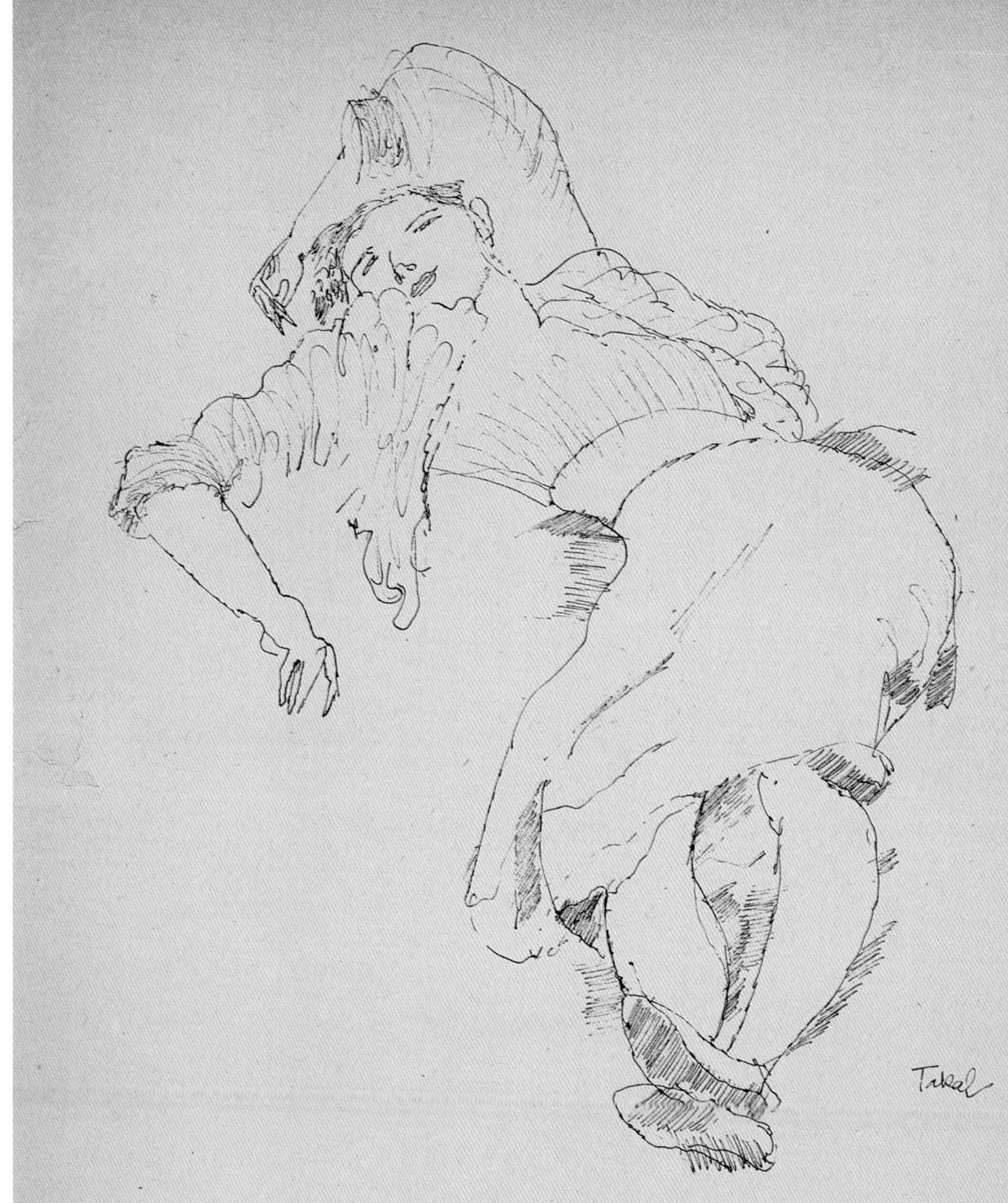

Reclining Woman
Paris, 1932
pen and india ink on tan paper
12 1/2 x 9 3/8 inches

27

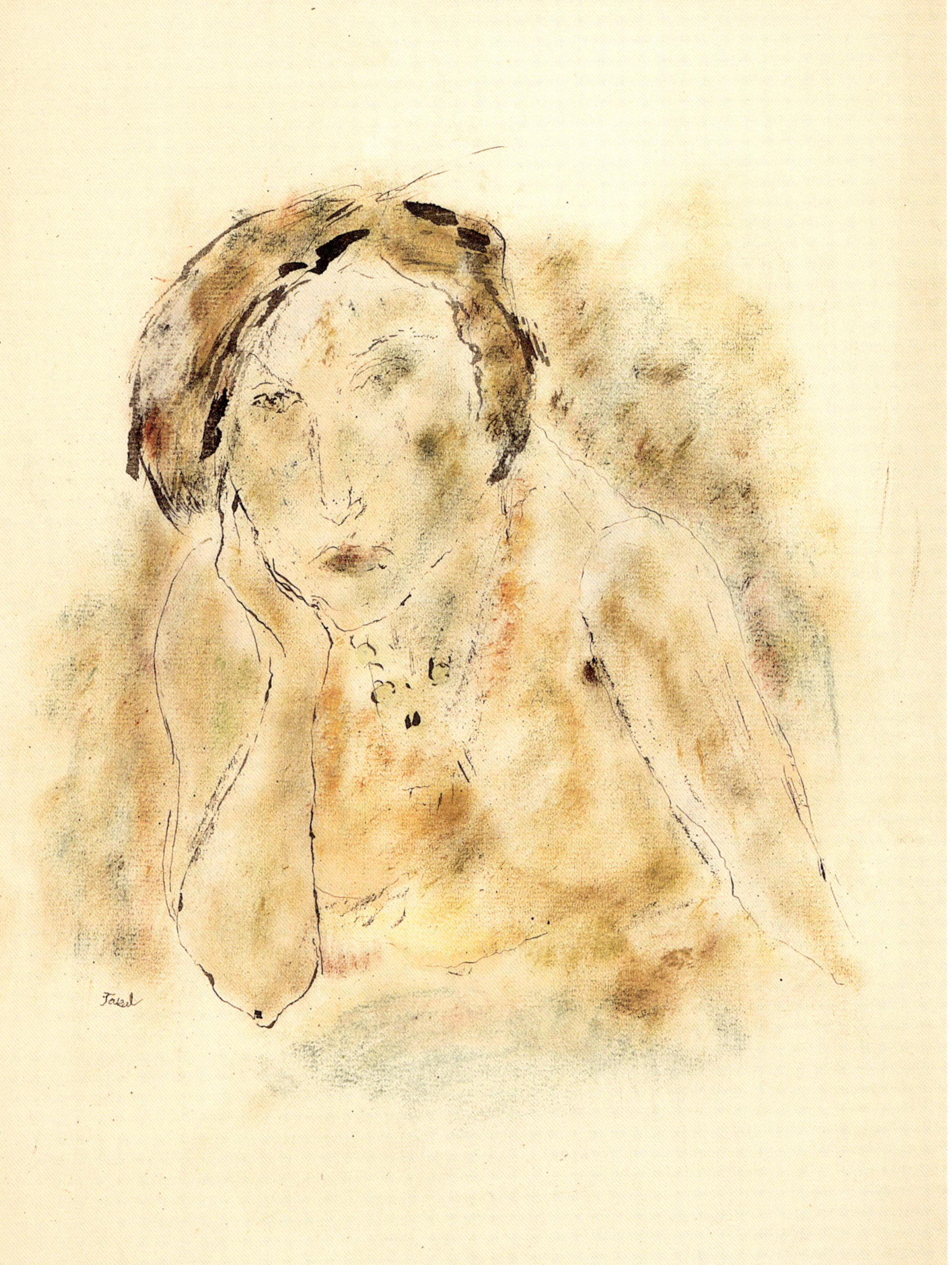

Woman Leaning on Hand
Paris, 1932
pen and india ink and pastel on paper
18 1/4 x 12 5/8 inches

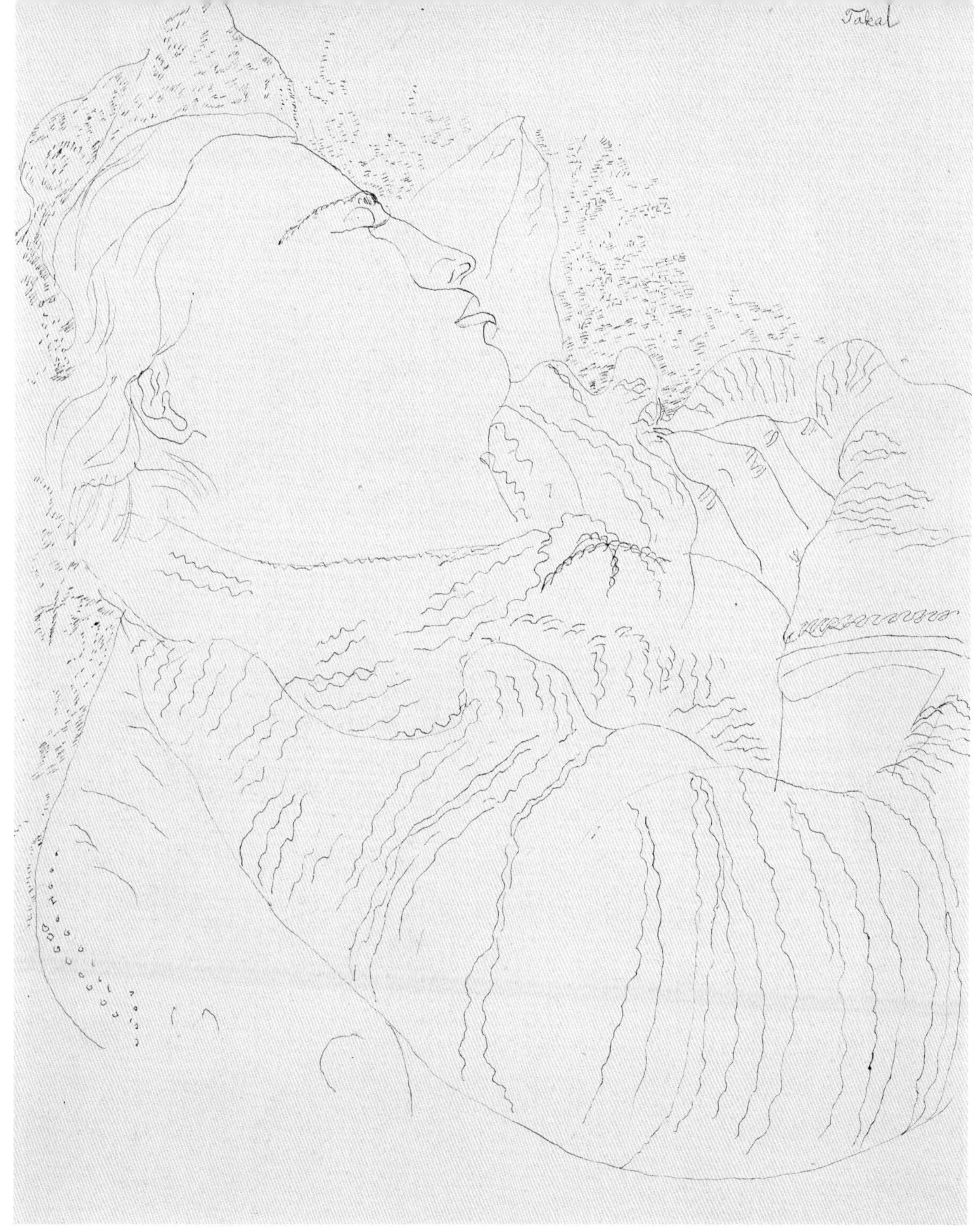

Woman Sleeping
Paris, 1933
pen and sepia ink on light tan paper
10 5/8 x 8 5/8 inches

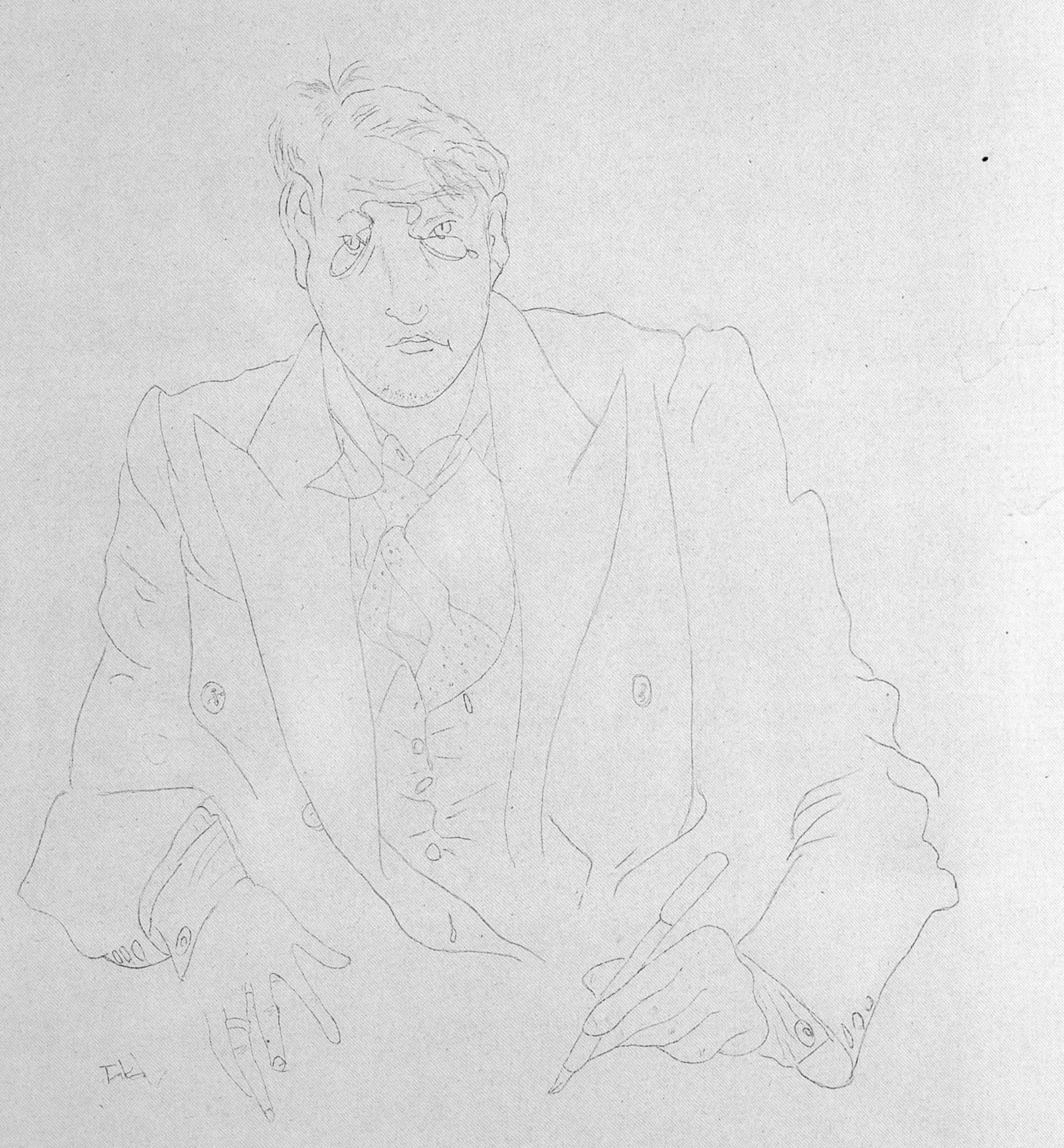

Ecrivain (The Writer)
1934
pen and india ink on light tan paper
13 3/4 x 11 inches
Arkansas Arts Center Foundation
Collection: Gift of Mrs. Peter Takal,
Geneva, Switzerland, 1996.

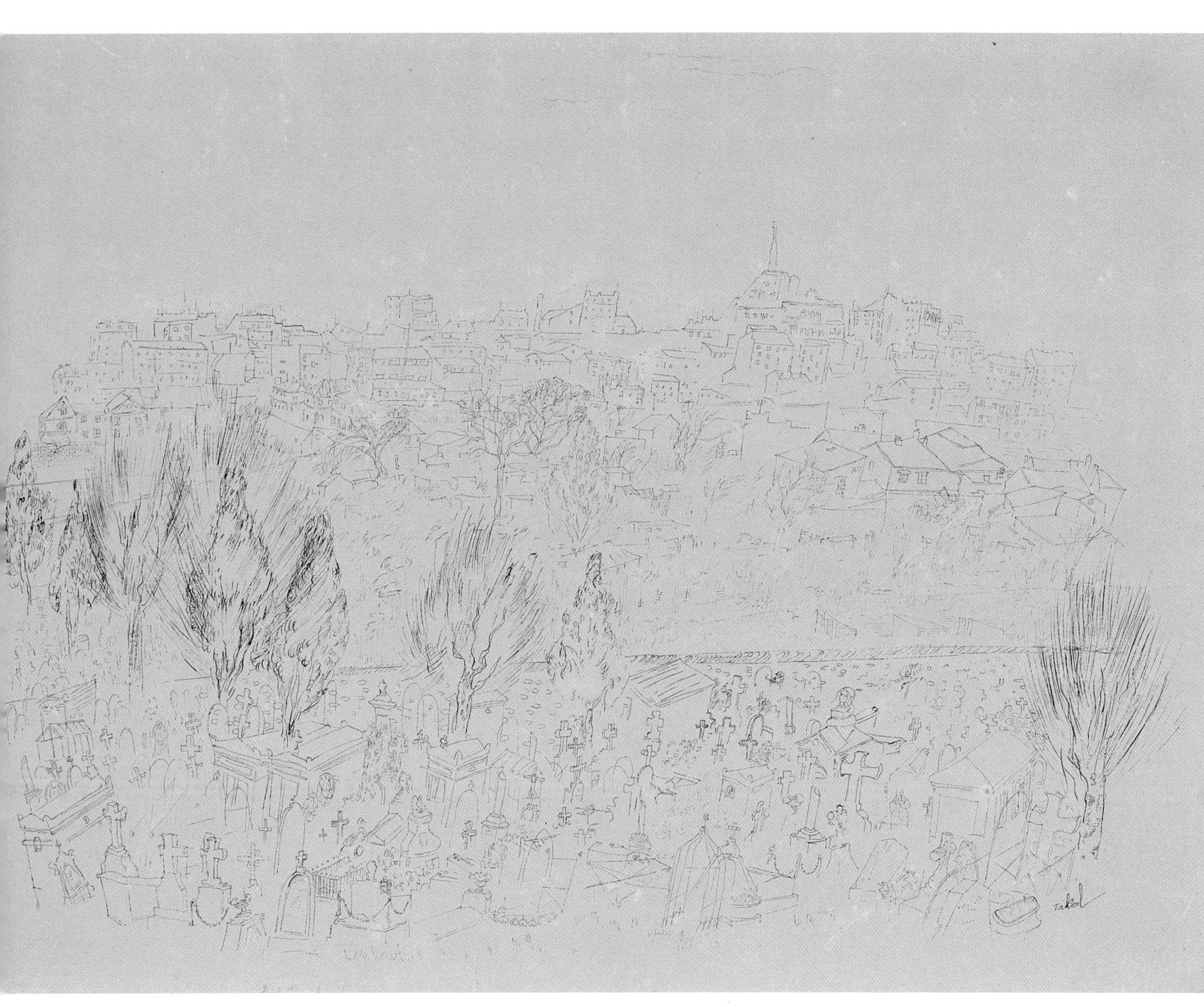

Cemetery
Kremlin-Bicêtre, 1935 or 1936
pen and india ink on heavy brown paper
17 1/8 x 21 5/8 inches

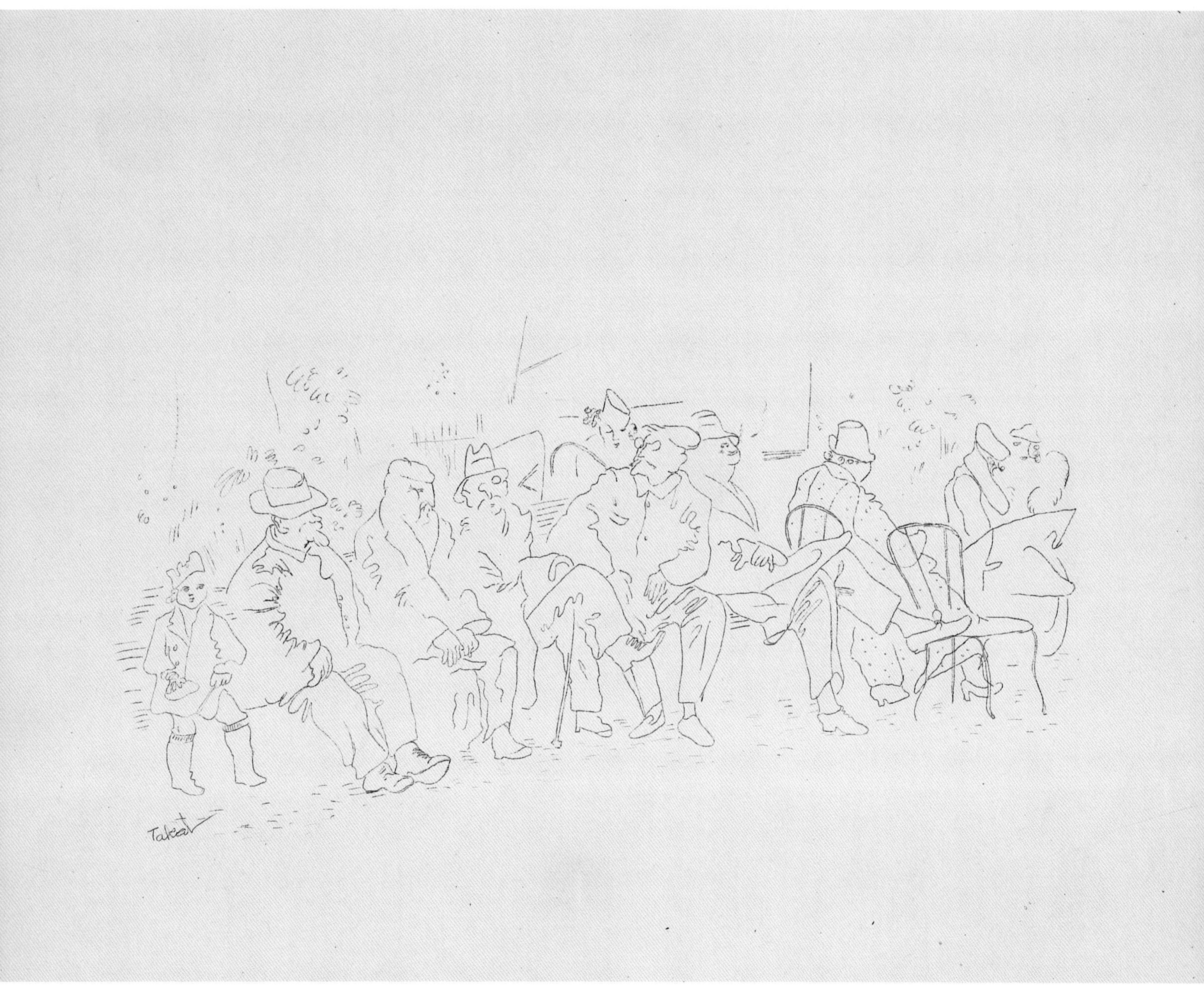

People in the Park
Paris, 1936
pen and india ink on paper
12 1/2 x 16 3/4 inches

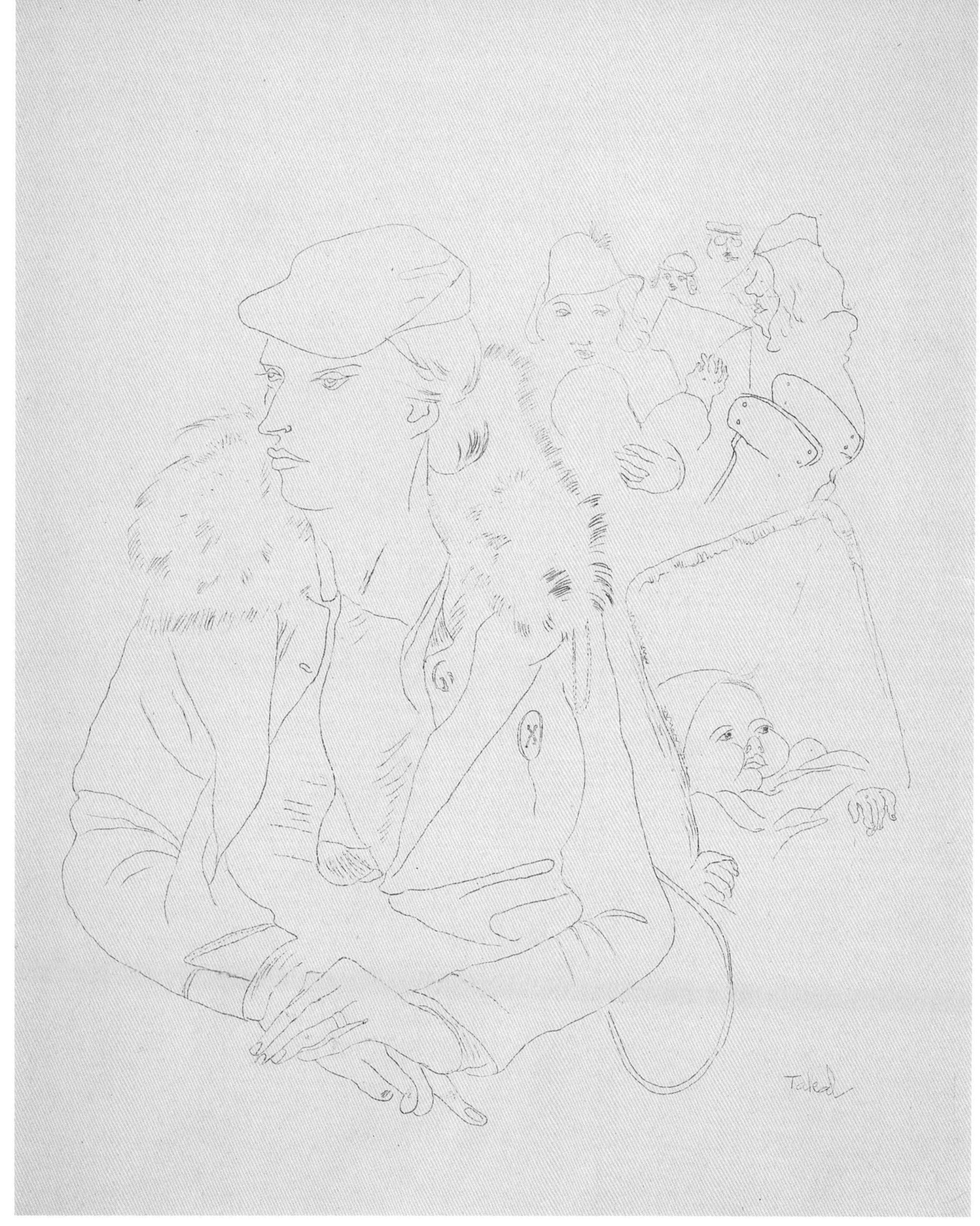

Mother with Baby
Paris, 1936
pen and india ink on tan paper
14 7/8 x 11 1/8 inches

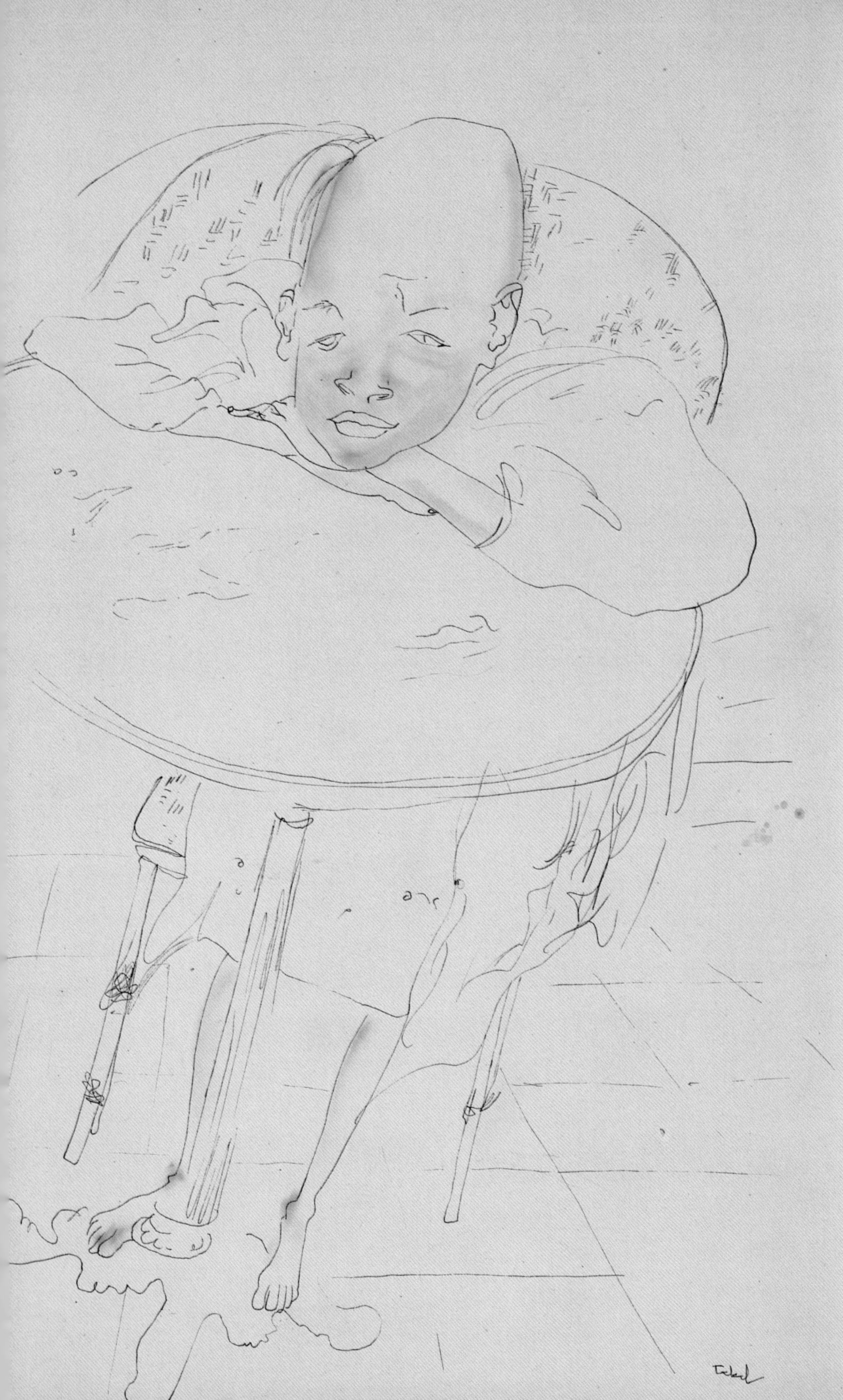

Little Boy at a Table
Morocco, 1937
pen and india ink with brown accents on mat board
17 5/8 x 11 1/8 inches

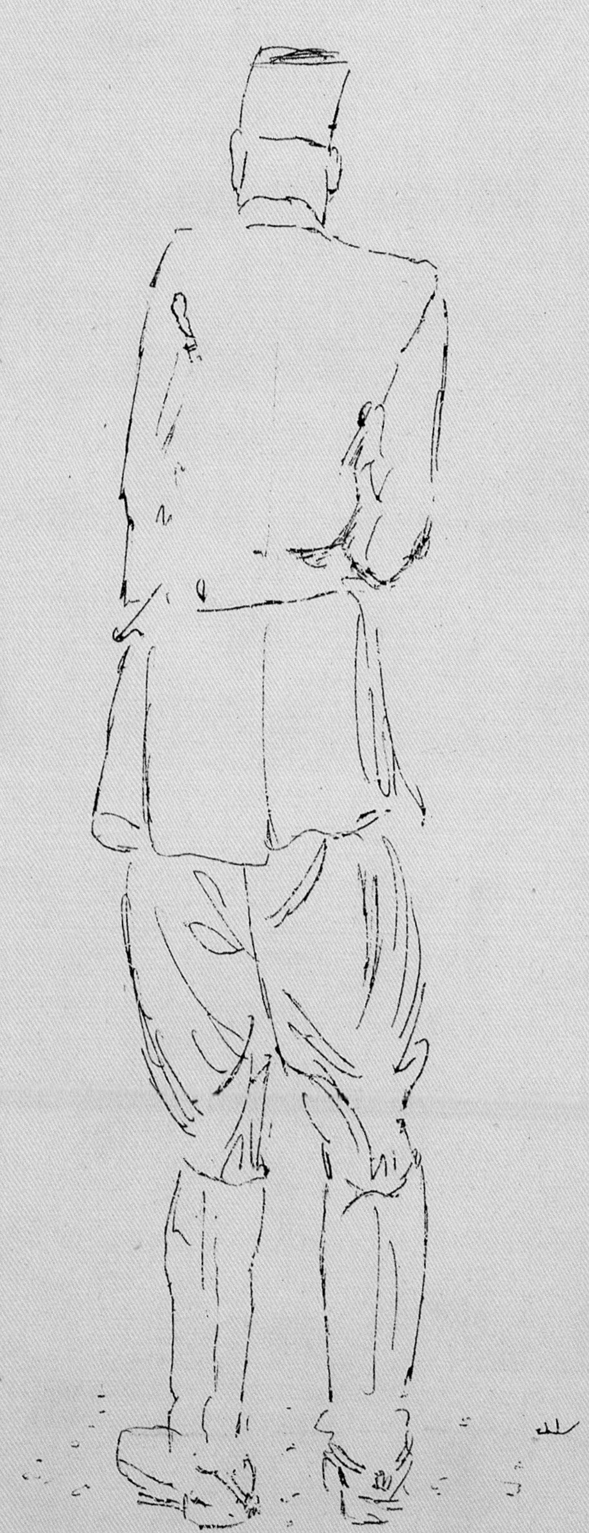

Legionnaire
Morocco, 1937
pen and india ink on paper
17 1/4 x 10 3/8 inches

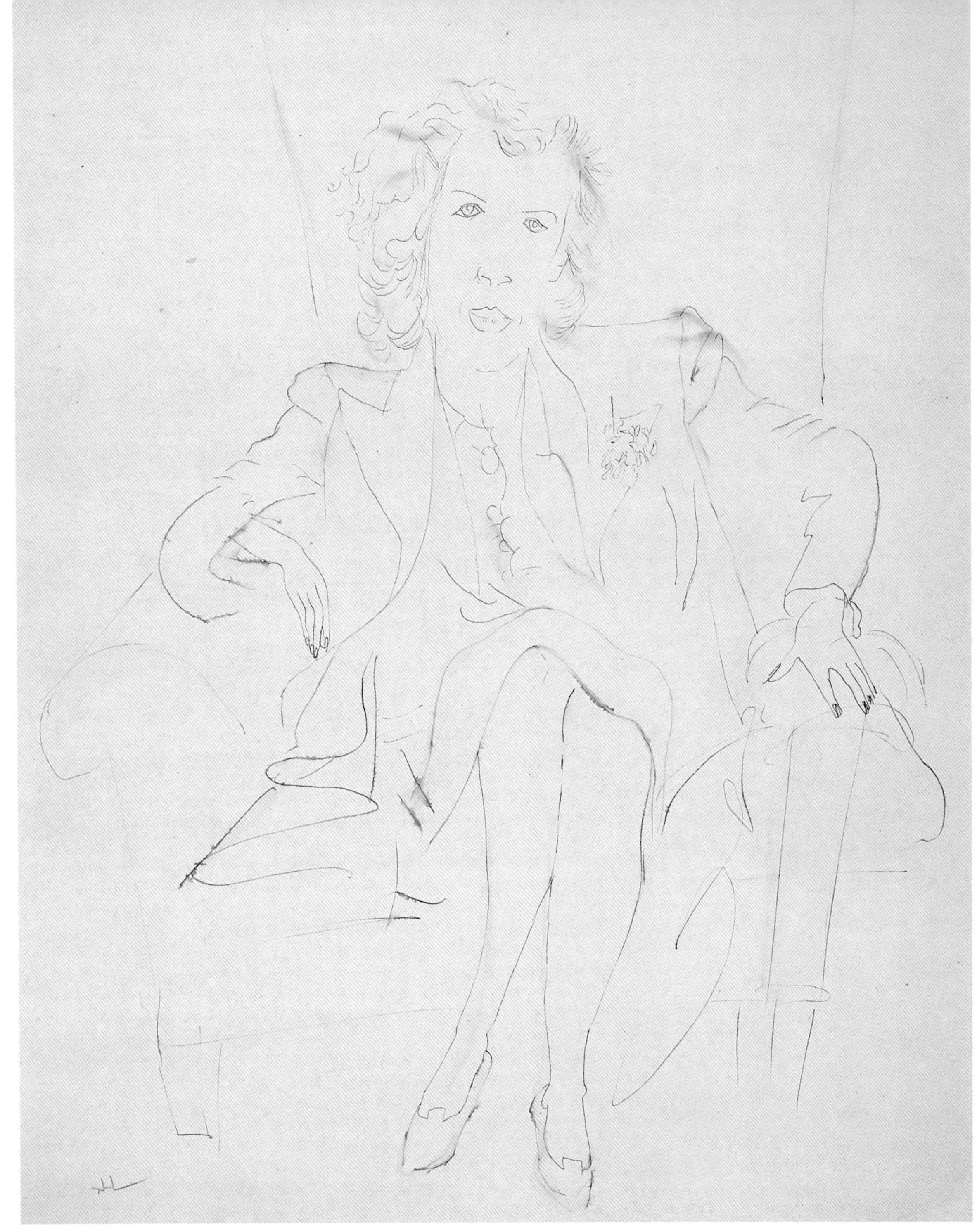

Woman in Armchair
France, 1937
pen and india ink with blue and brown accents on paper
22 1/8 x 16 1/2 inches

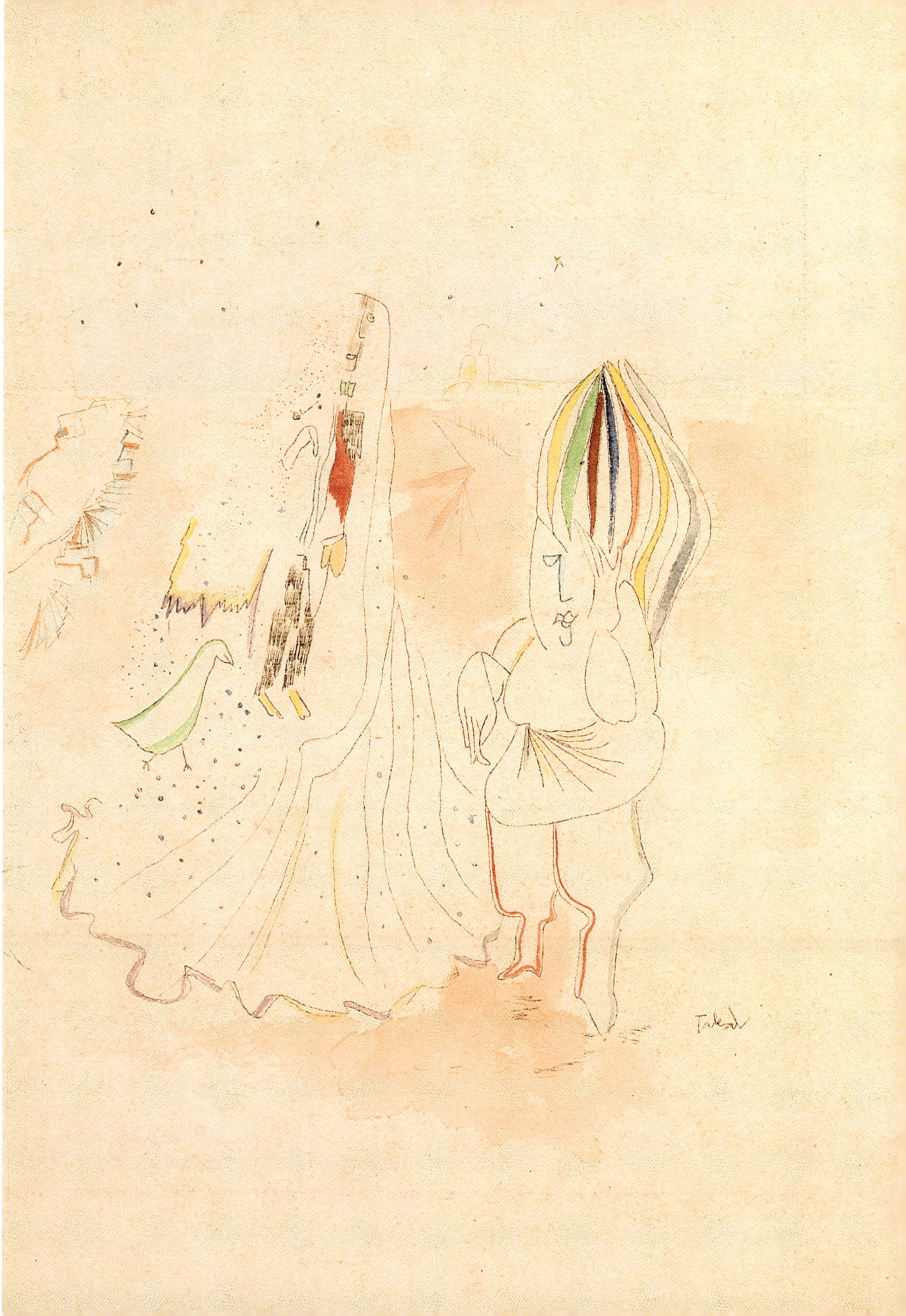

Fantasy
Paris, 1938
pen and sepia ink and watercolor on paper
10 1/4 x 6 7/8 inches

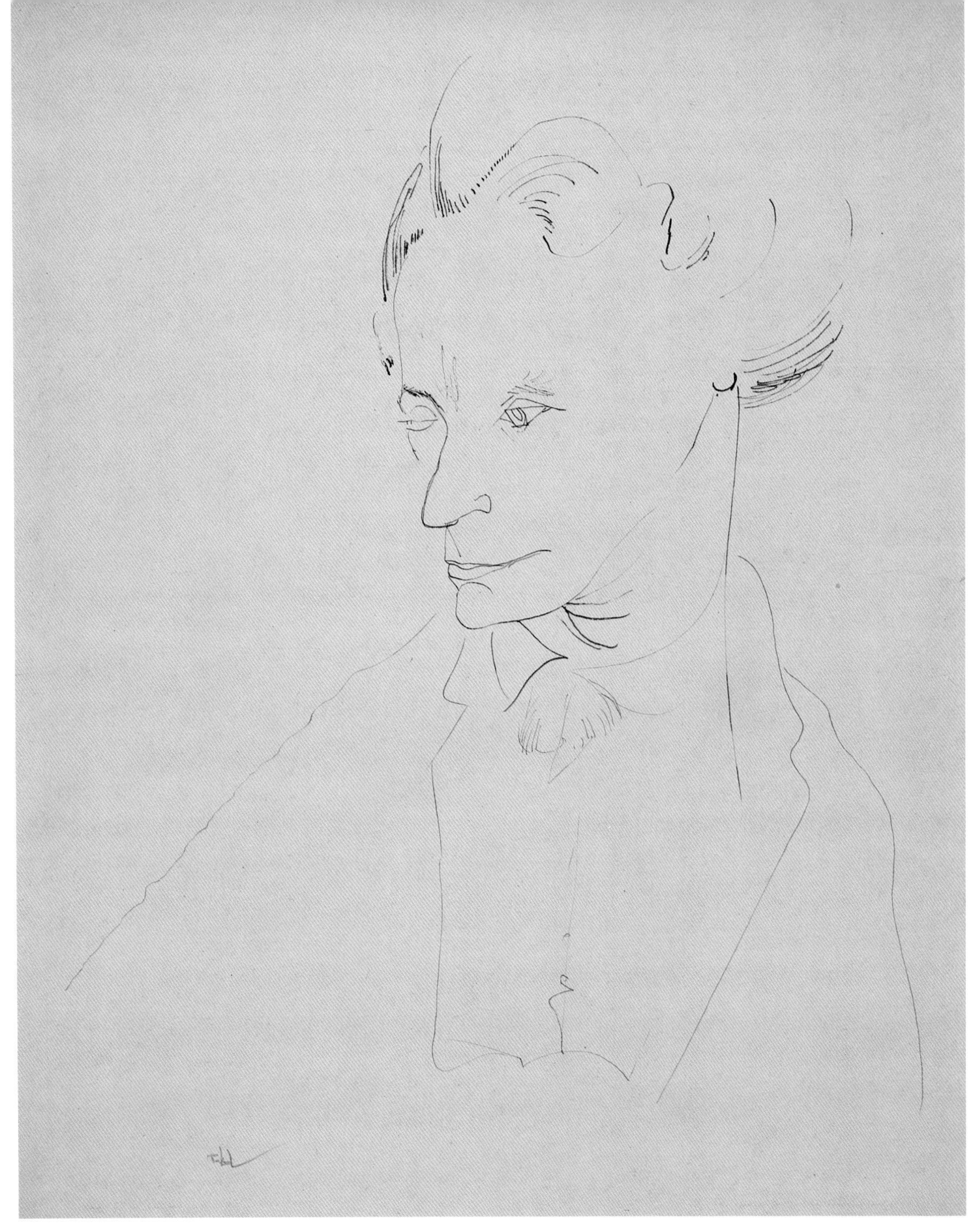

Portrait
Chicago, 1940
pen and india ink on paper
21 5/8 x 17 1/8 inches

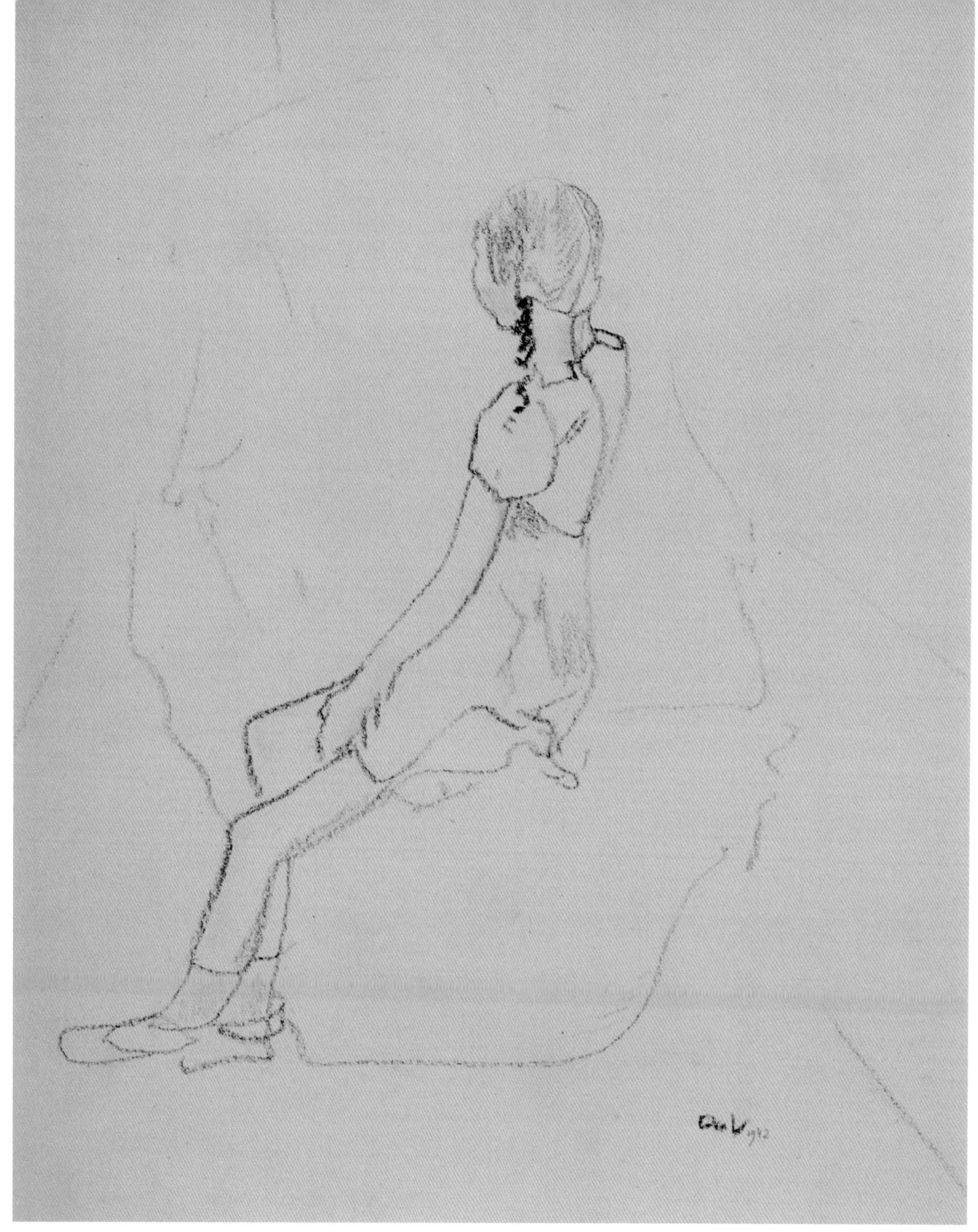

Anne Sitting on Daybed
New York, 1942
heavy graphite pencil on brown paper
19 x 15 1/2 inches

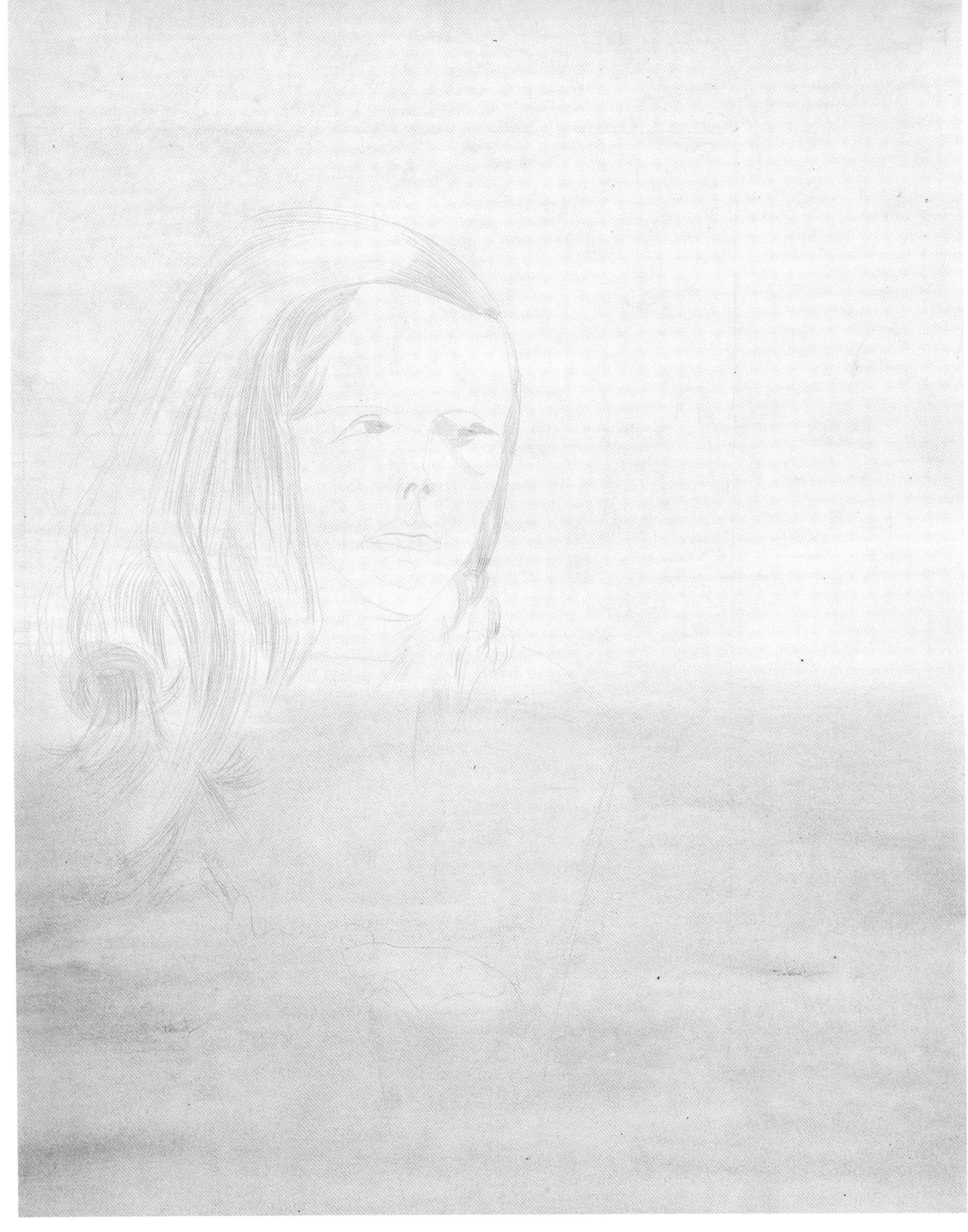

Head of a Girl
New York, 1943
silverpoint on prepared paper
17 1/2 x 14 1/4 inches

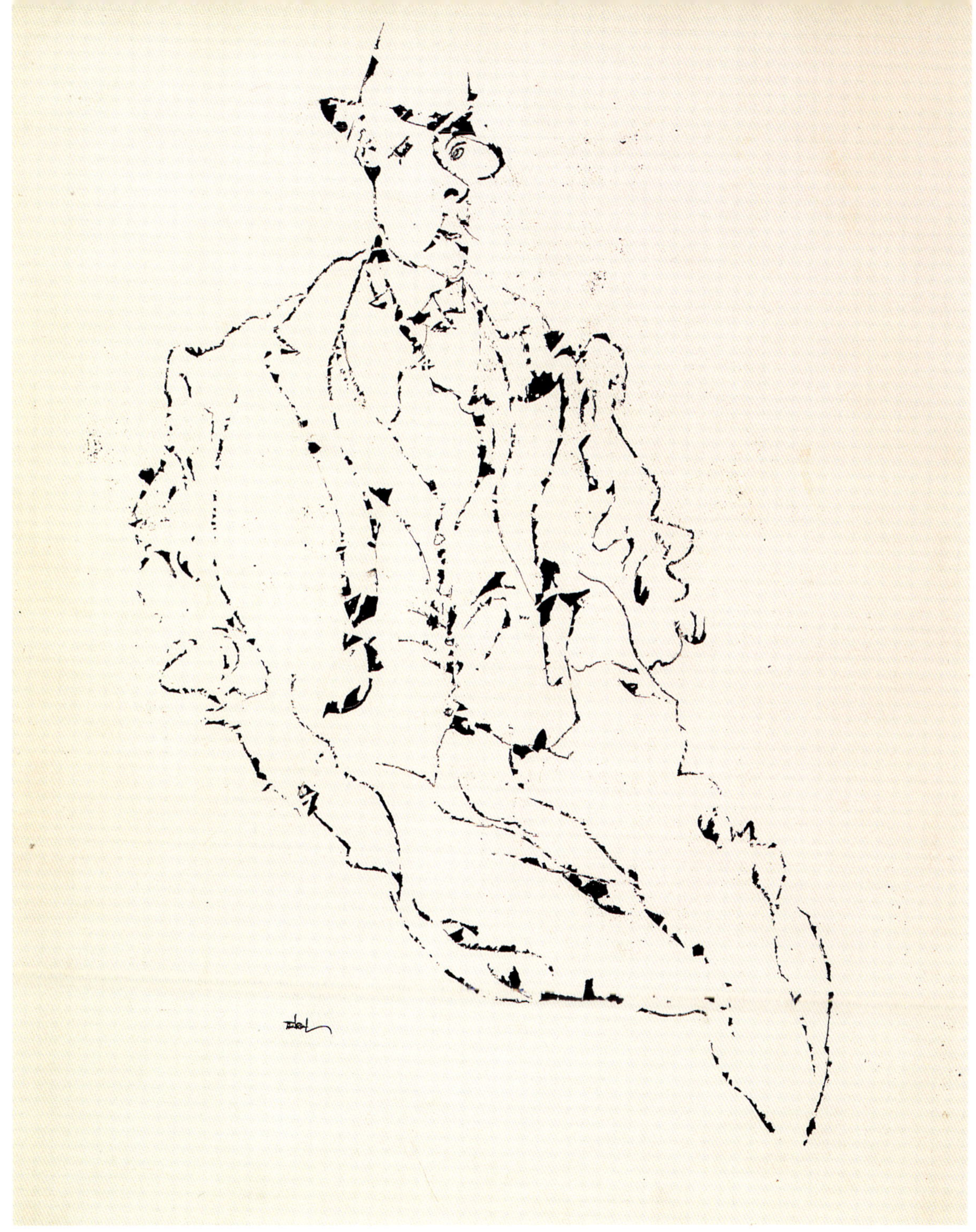

Dandy
New York, 1945
pen and india ink on paper
21 3/8 x 16 3/4 inches

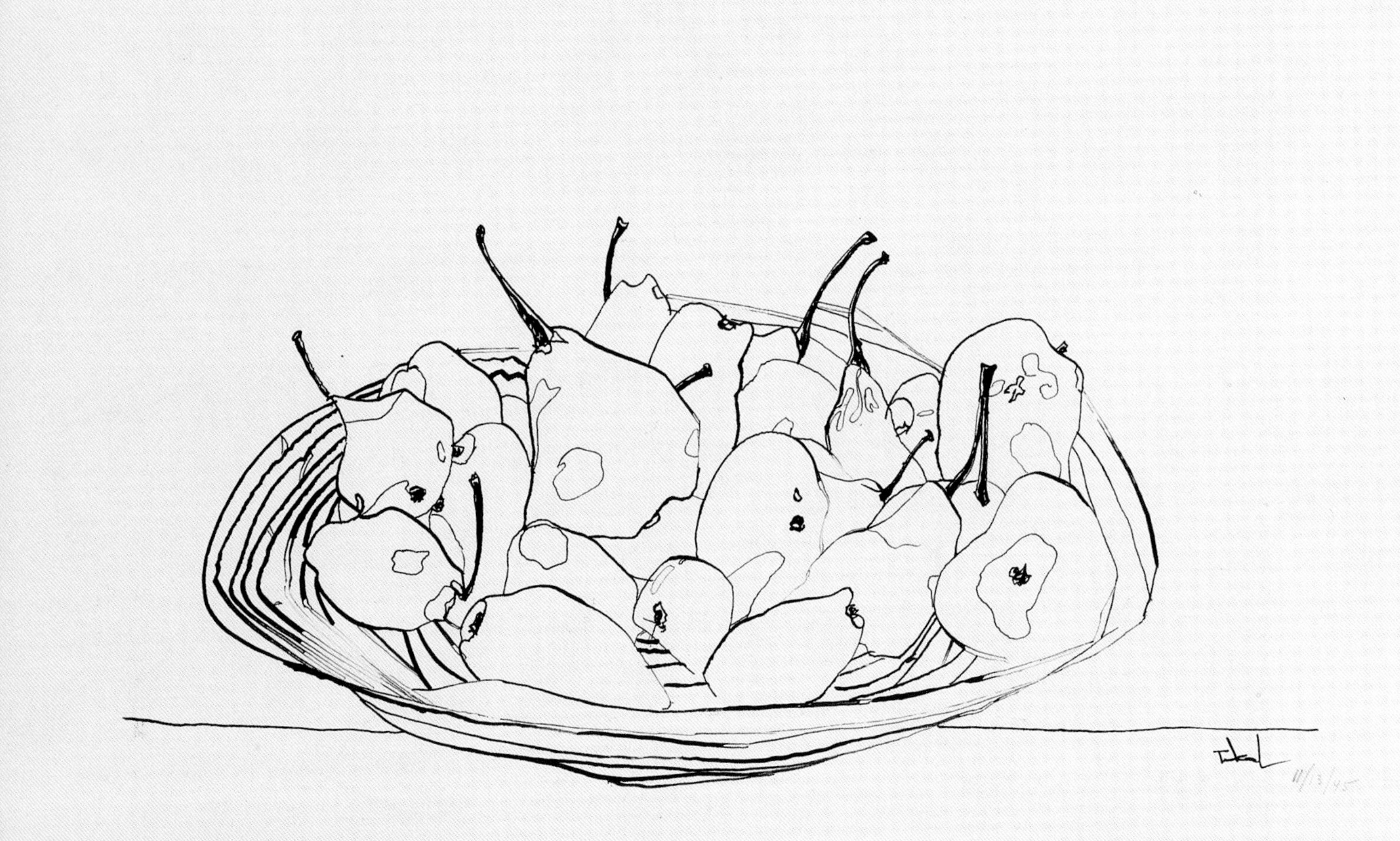

Dish with Pears
Saylorsburg, Pennsylvania, 1945
pen and india ink on paper
15 1/8 x 22 1/8 inches

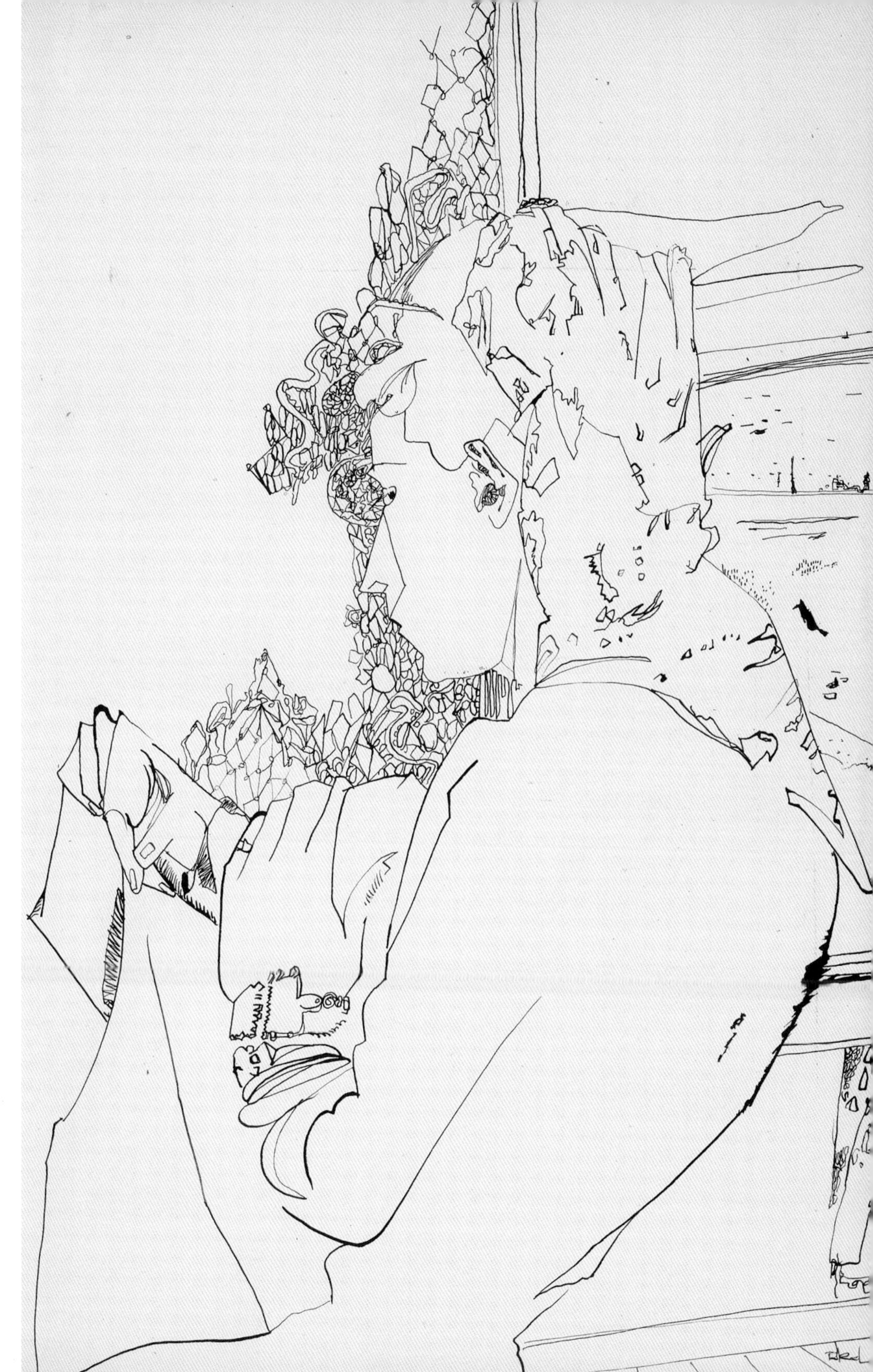

Woman Near Window
Dieppe, France, 1947
pen and india ink on paper
22 1/8 x 14 3/8 inches

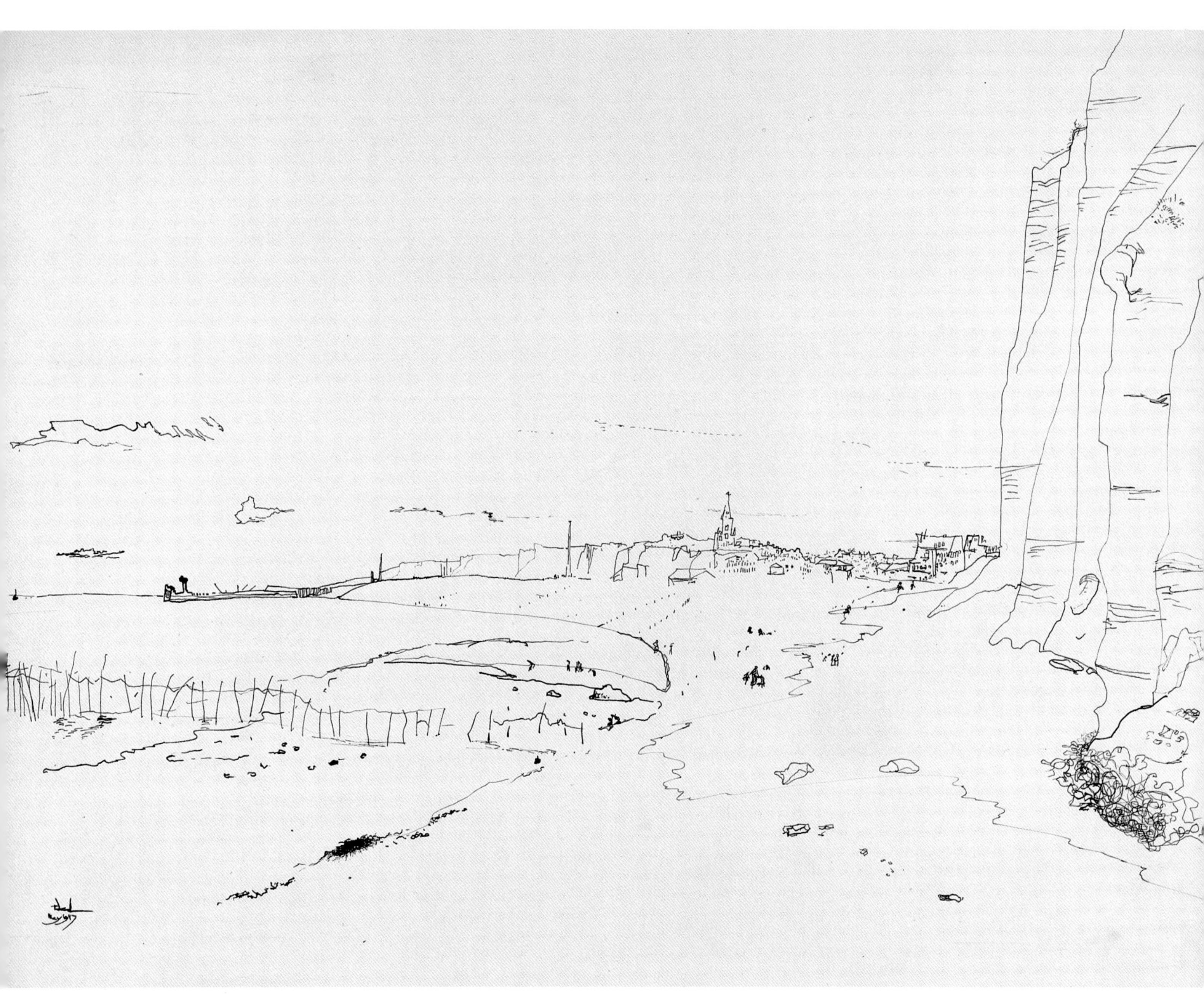

Beach
Dieppe, France, 1947
pen and india ink on paper
15 7/8 x 22 1/8 inches

44

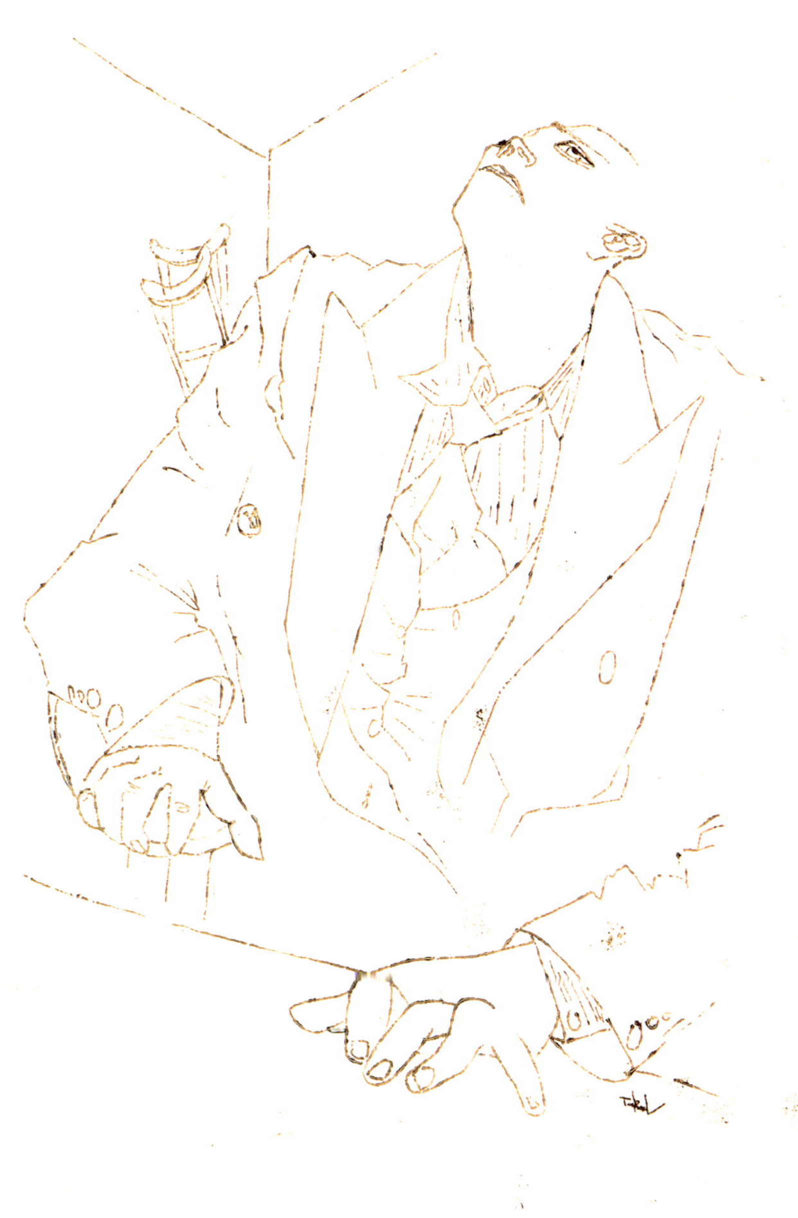

Man Looking Upward
New York, 1947
pen and sepia ink on paper
15 5/8 x 11 3/4 inches

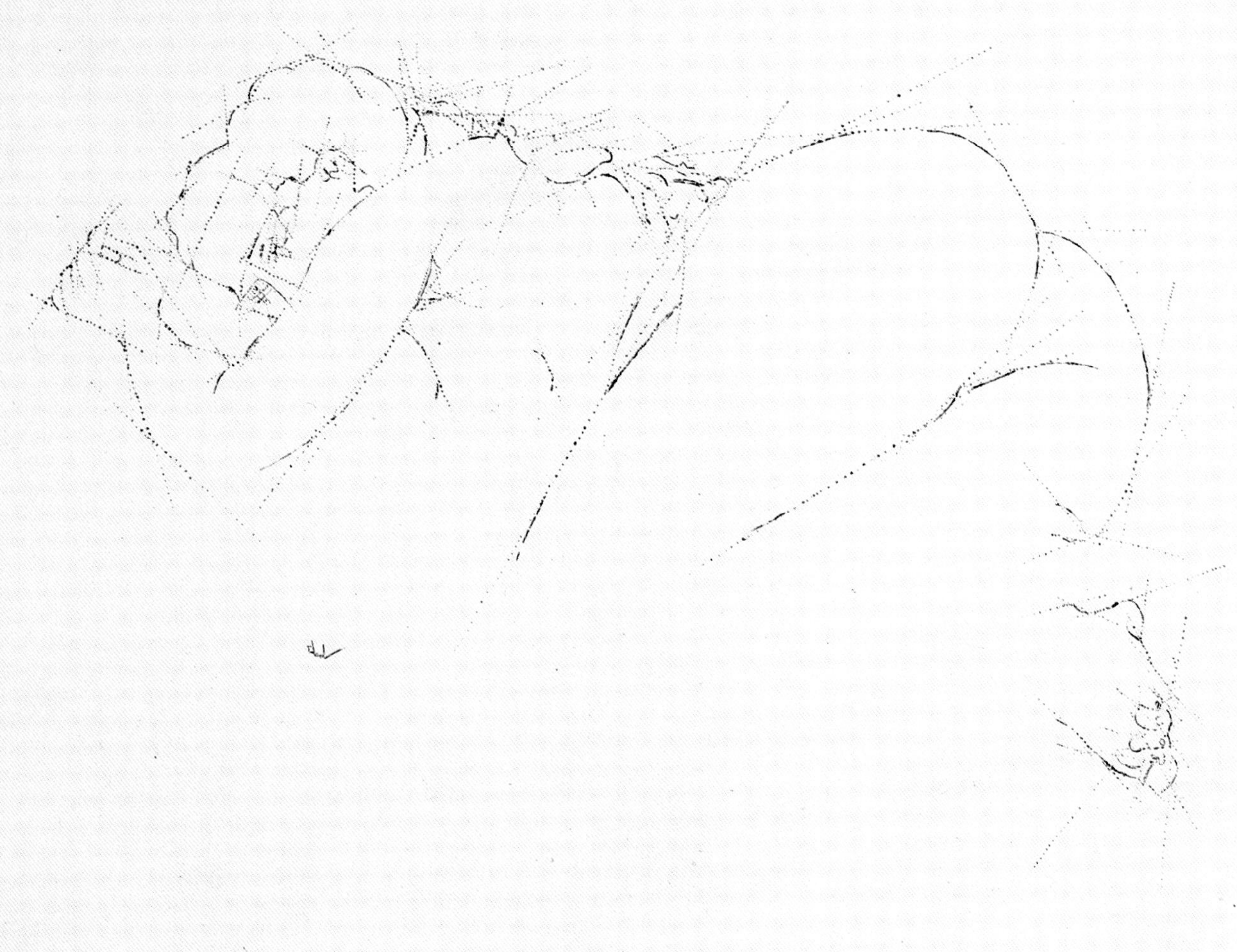

Reclining Nude
New York, 1950
dotted india ink on paper
10 7/8 x 16 1/8 inches

46

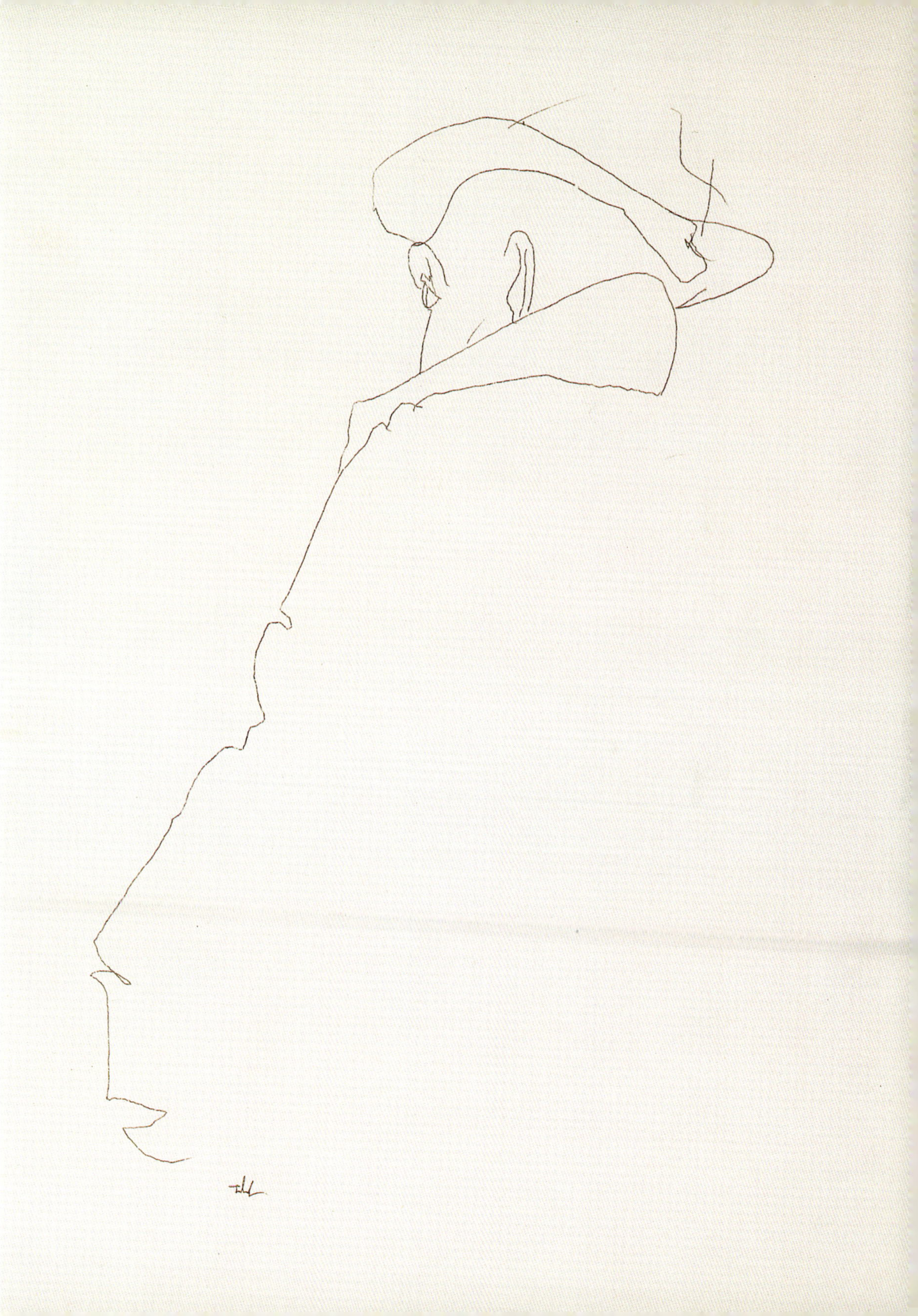

Subway Rider
New York, 1954
pen and india ink on paper
14 x 11 1/8 inches

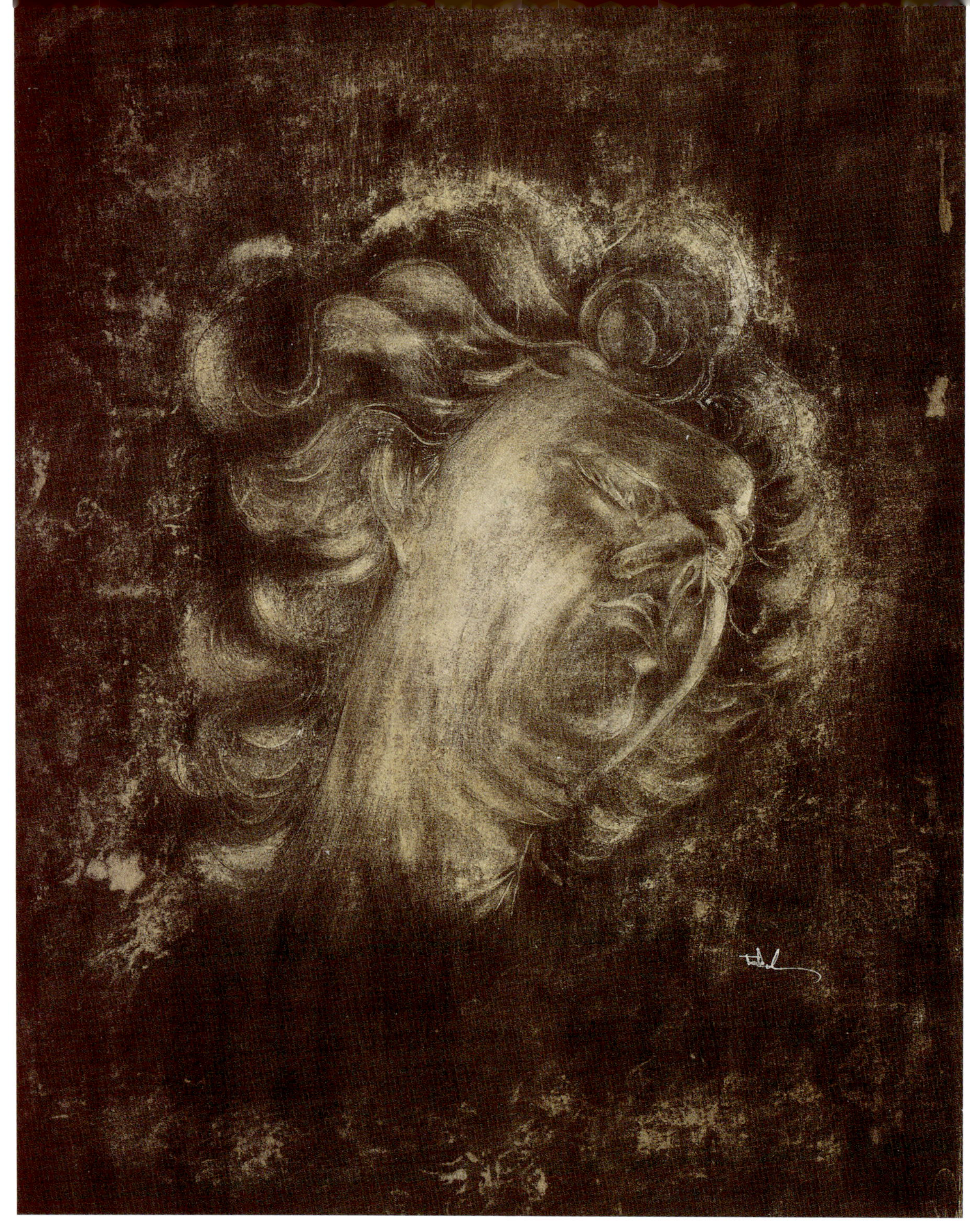

Head of a Sleeping Woman
New York, 1954
mixed media on paper
22 3/8 x 17 5/8 inches

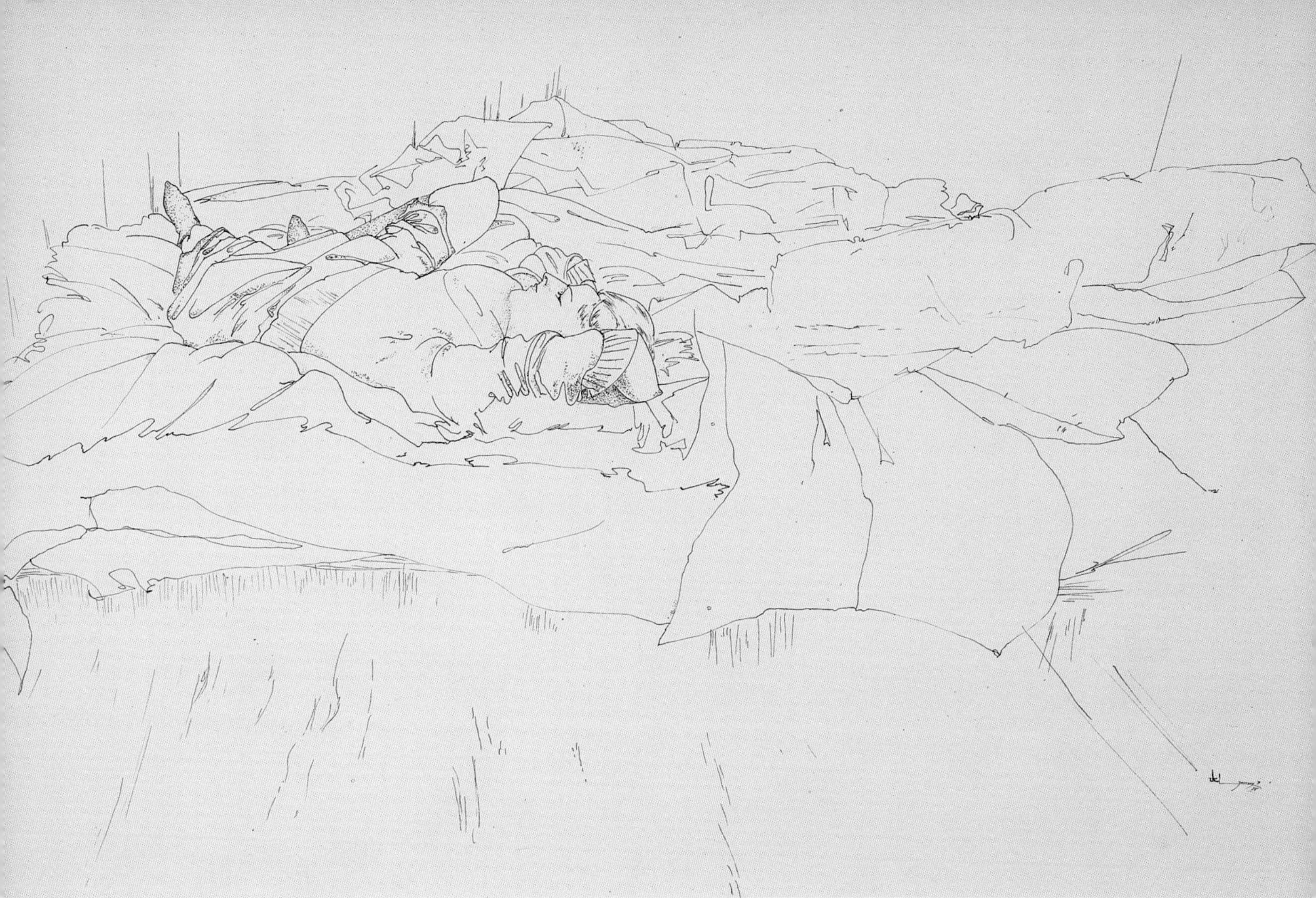

Girl on Bed
1955
pen and india ink on paper
20 x 28 inches

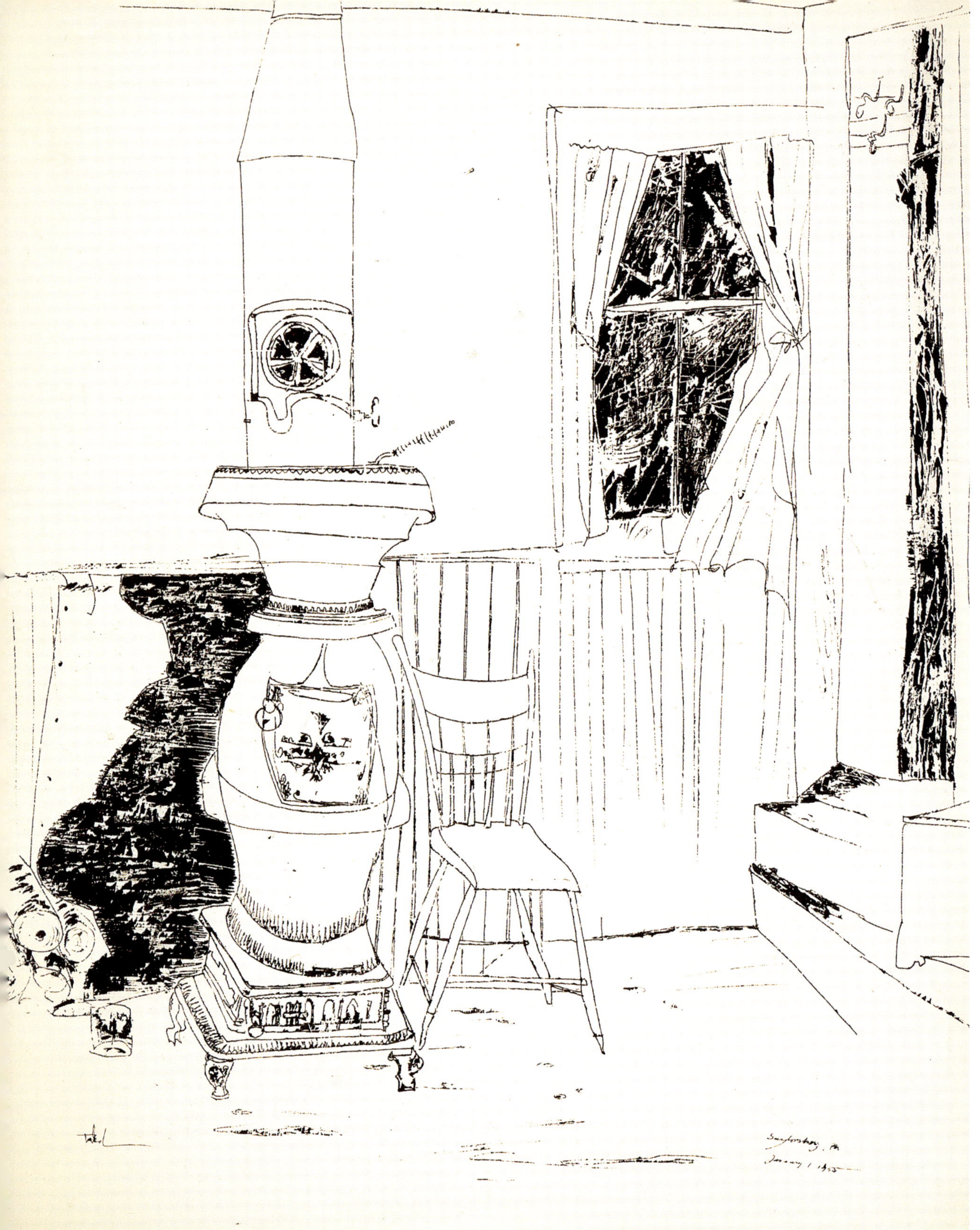

Wood Stove and Chair
Saylorsburg, Pennsylvania, 1955
pen and india ink on paper
28 1/2 x 22 1/2 inches

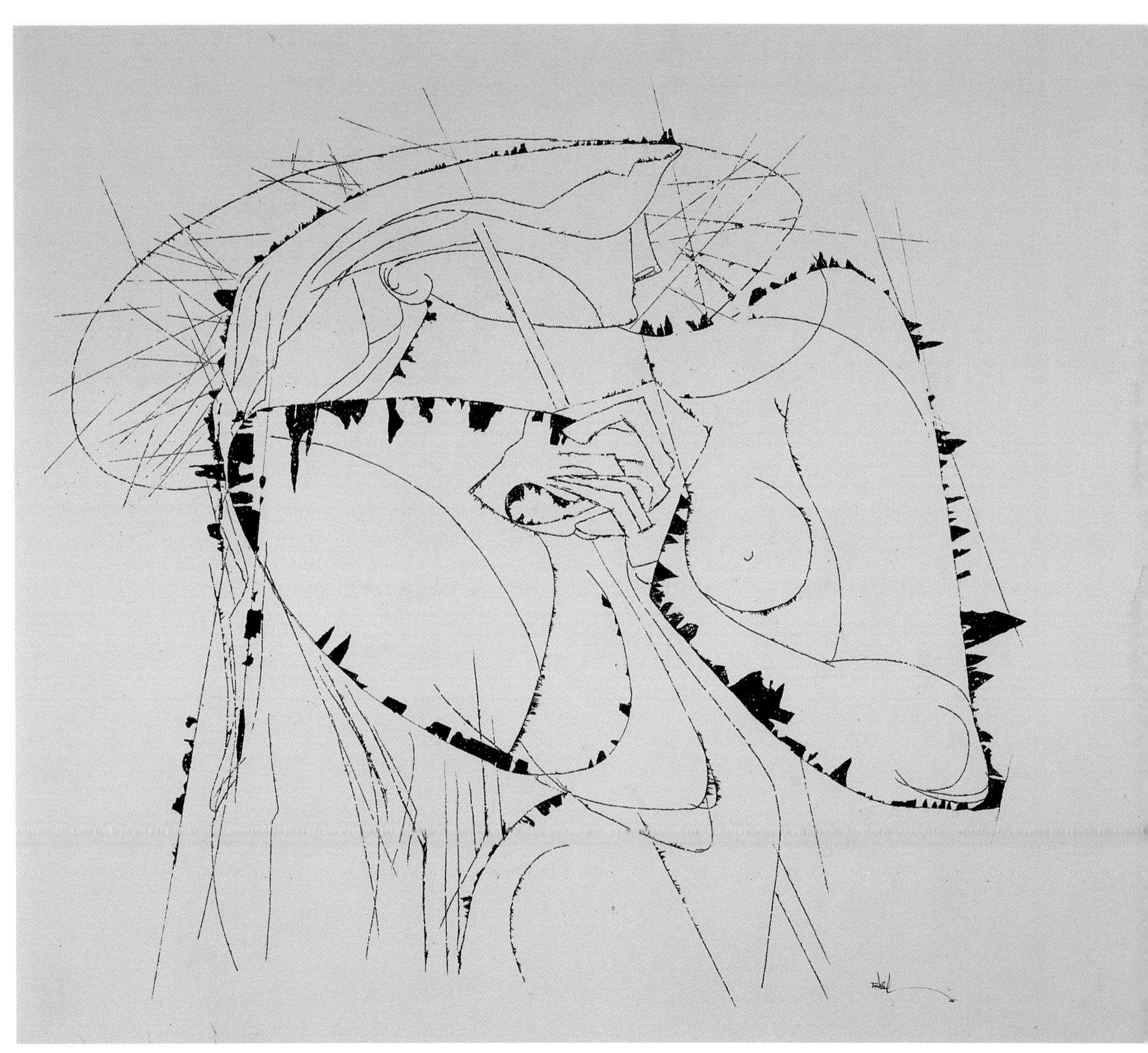

Nude with Parasol
1955
pen and india ink on mat board
29 7/8 x 35 3/4 inches

51

Tunnel
New York, 1956
pen and india ink on paper
35 1/4 x 26 1/2 inches

53

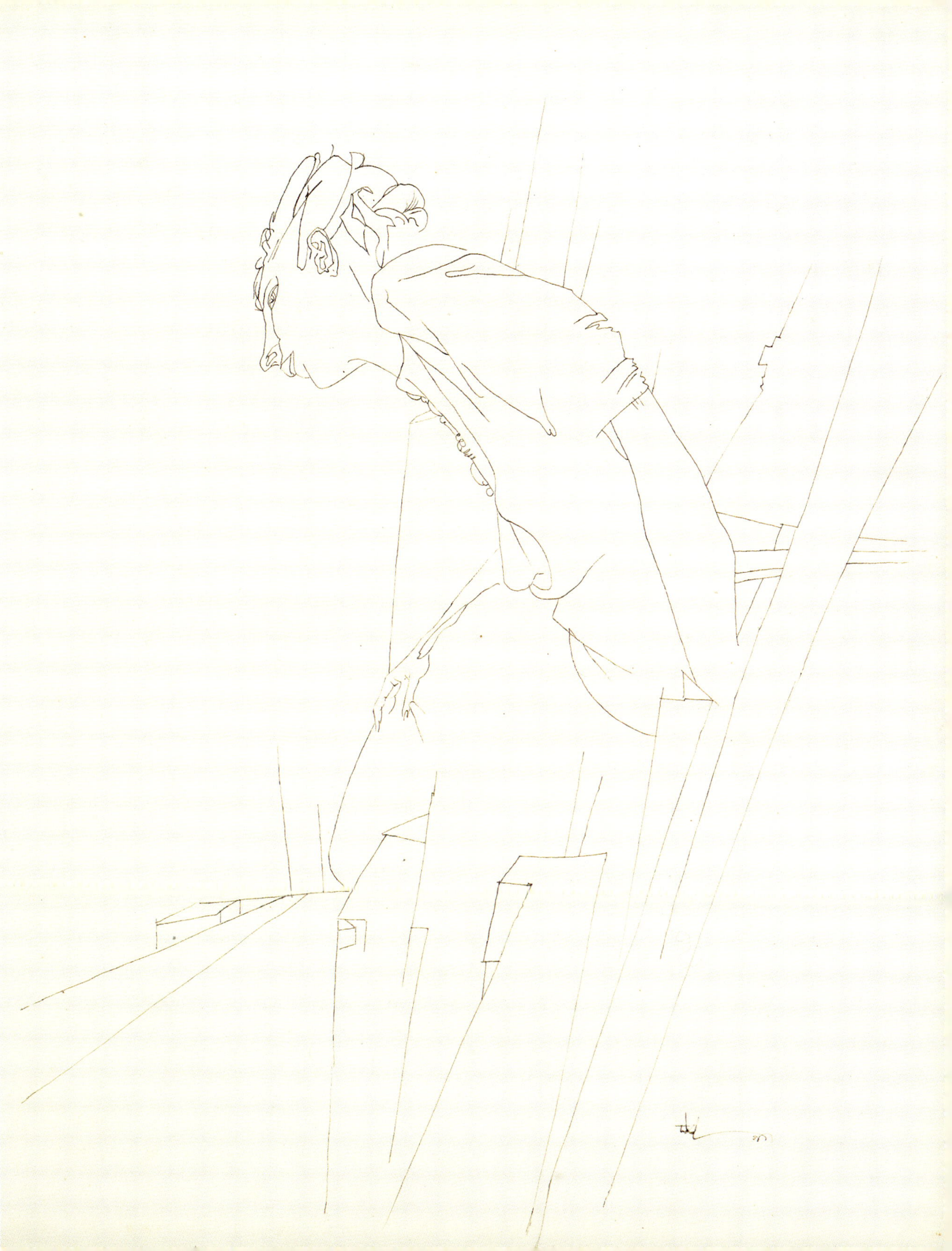

Creek in Forest
Nevada, 1956
pen and india ink on paper
24 3/4 x 19 inches

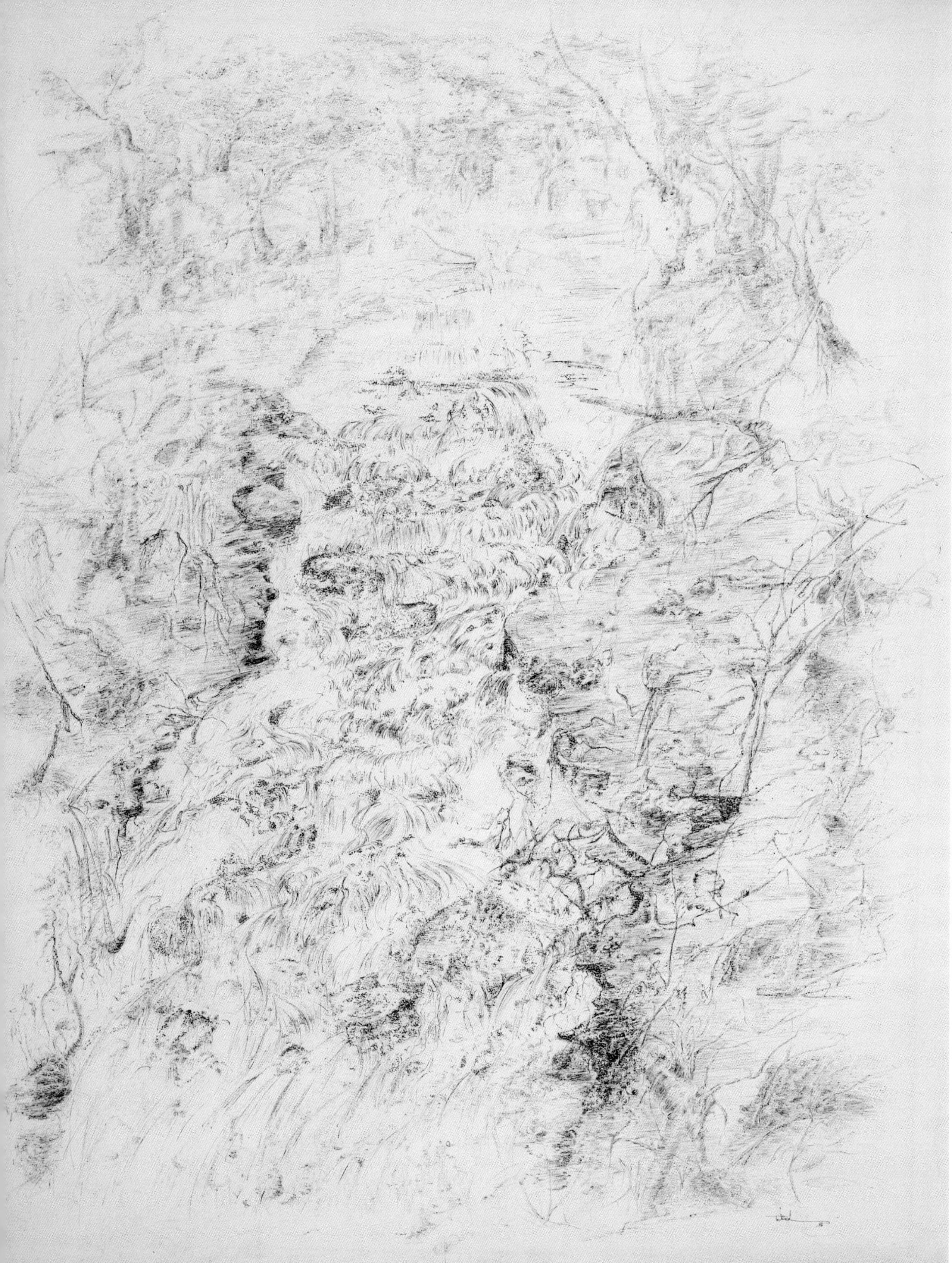

54

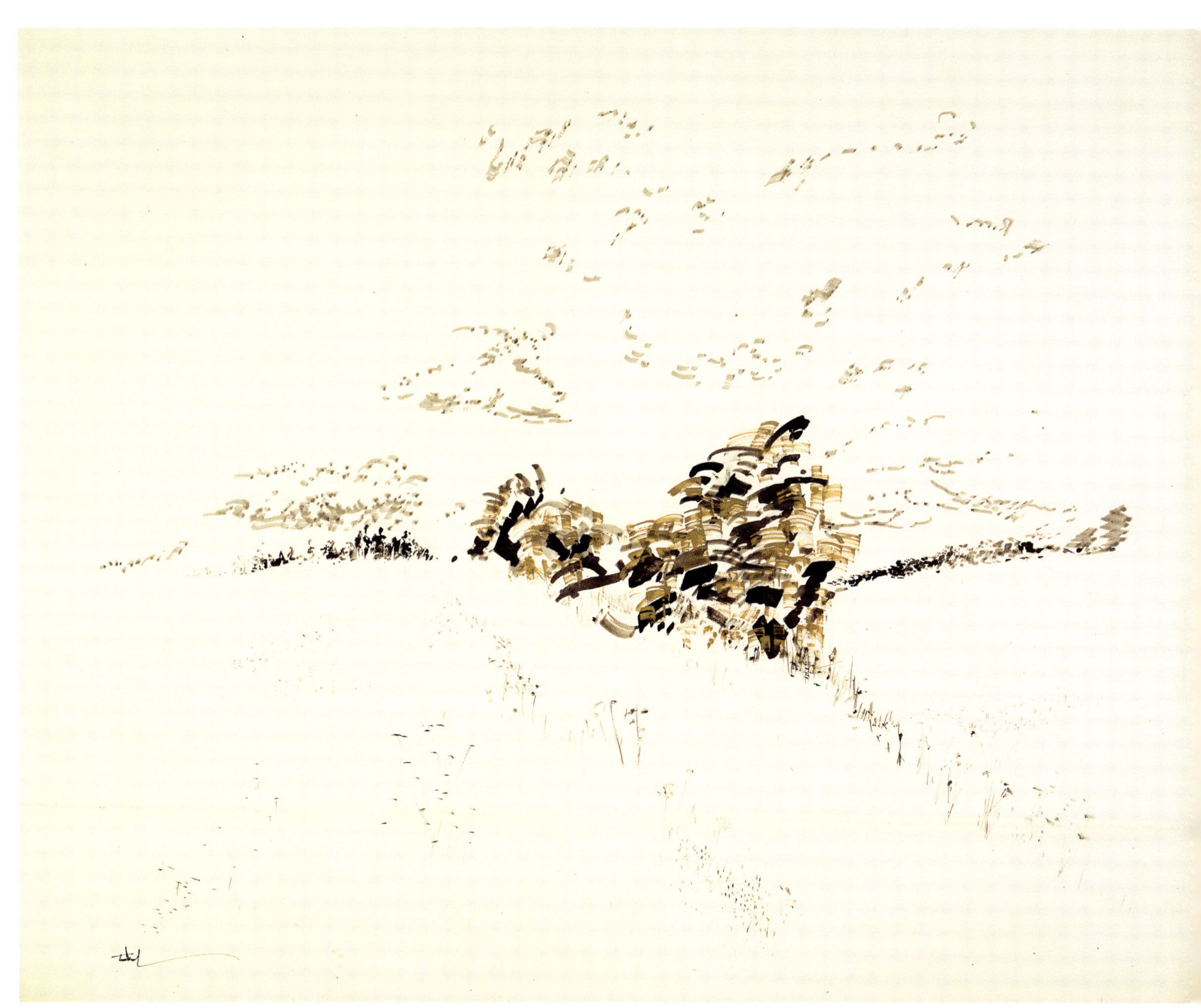

Road and Woods
Saylorsburg, Pennsylvania, 1957
reed pen and brush and india ink with ochre accents on paper
22 x 27 1/2 inches

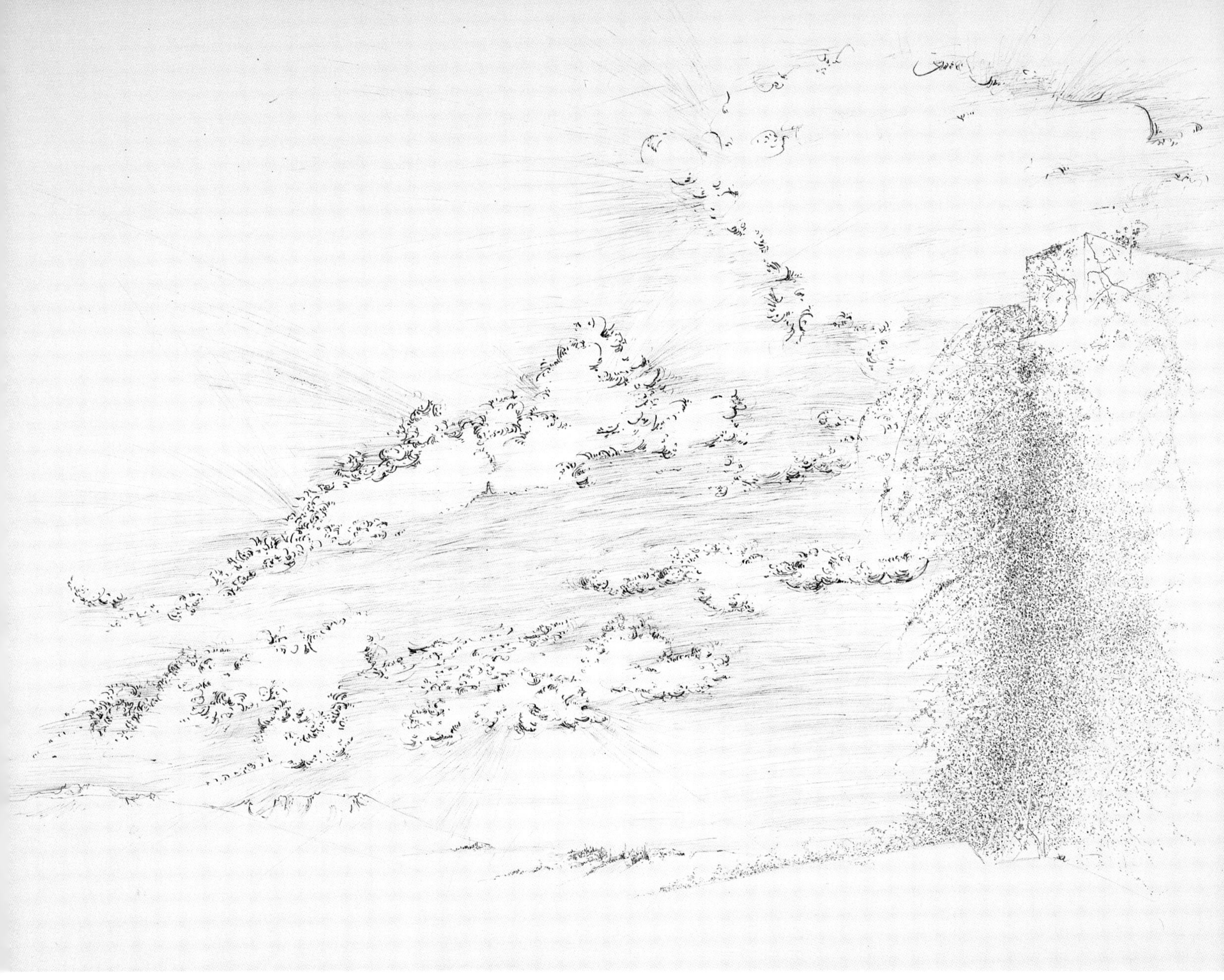

Flowering Vine and Clouds
Mexico, 1959
pen and india ink and sepia ink on paper
22 7/8 x 30 5/8 inches

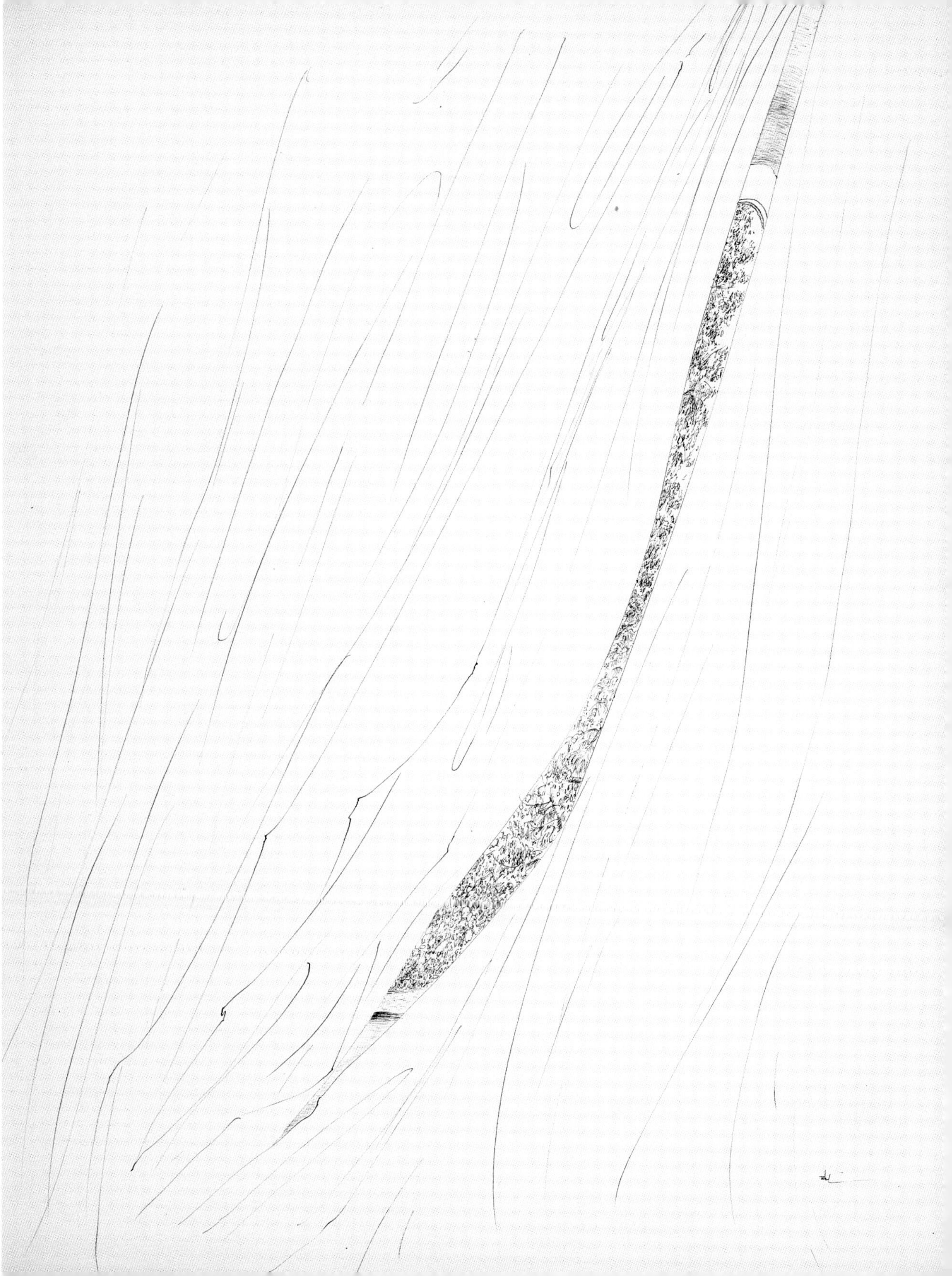

View Through Curtains
Mexico, 1959
pen and india ink on paper
28 1/2 x 22 1/2 inches

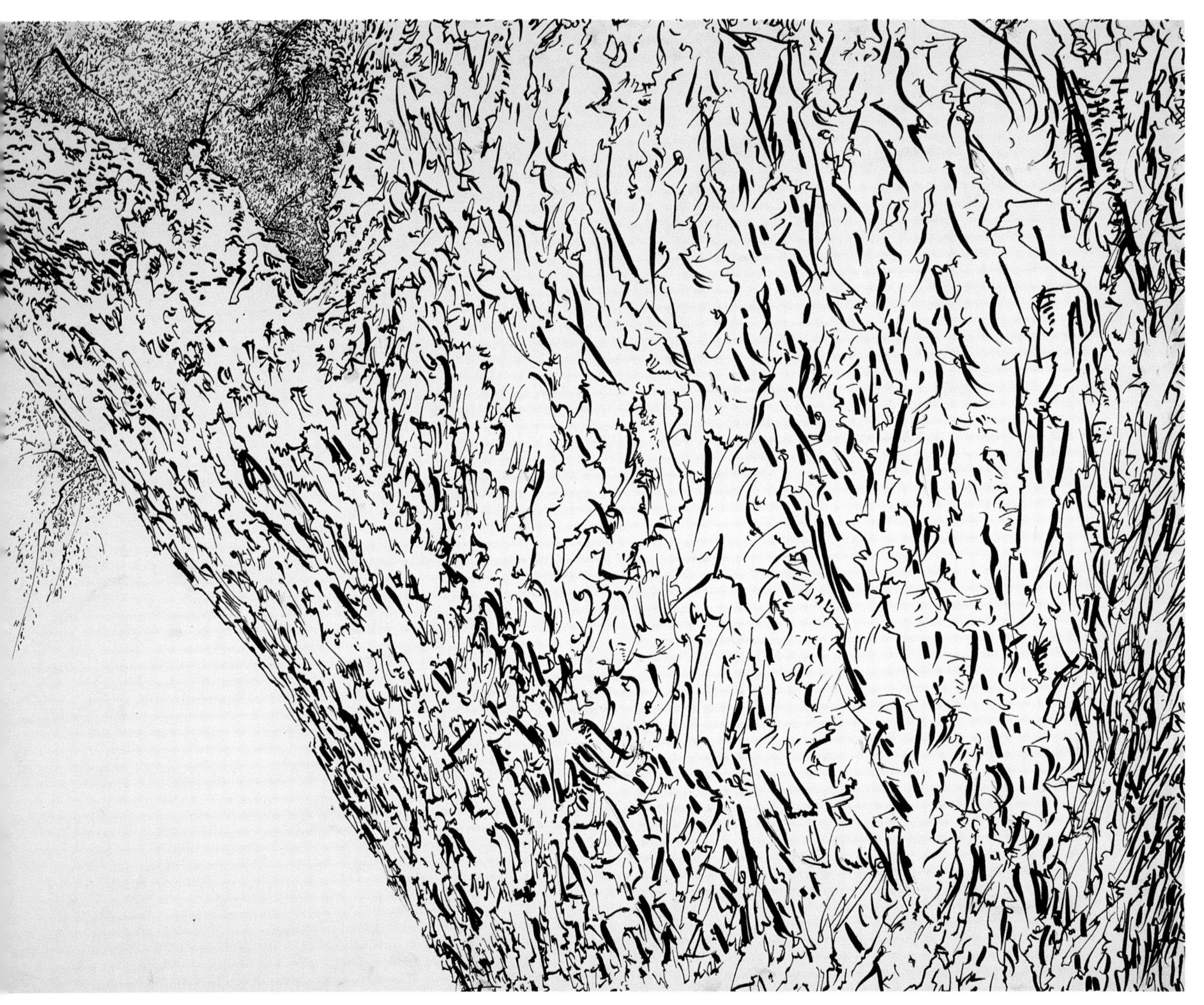

Tree Bark
Mexico, 1959
pen and india ink on paper
23 1/8 x 29 inches

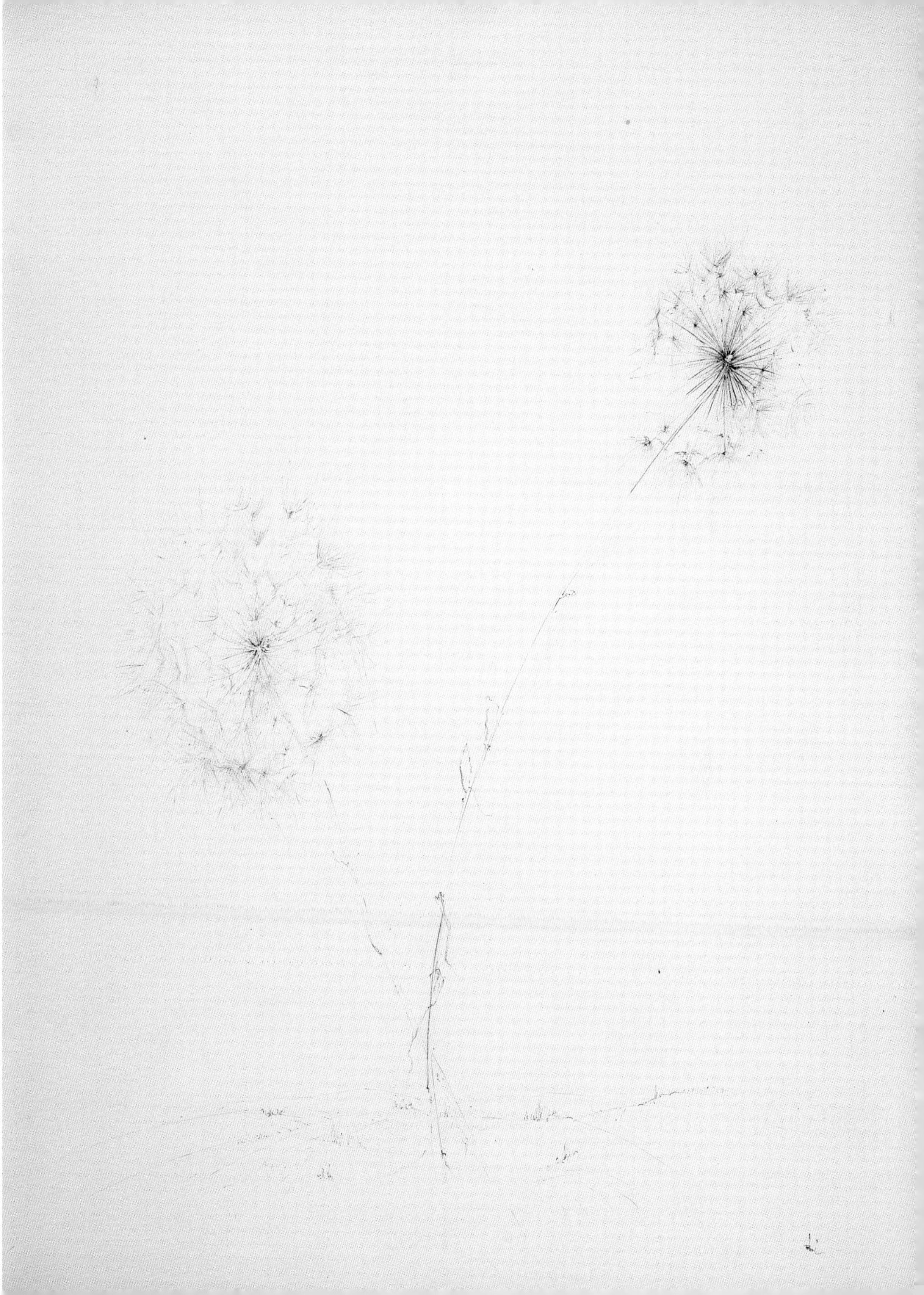

Dandelions
near Florence, 1960
pen and india ink on paper
39 3/8 x 28 3/4 inches

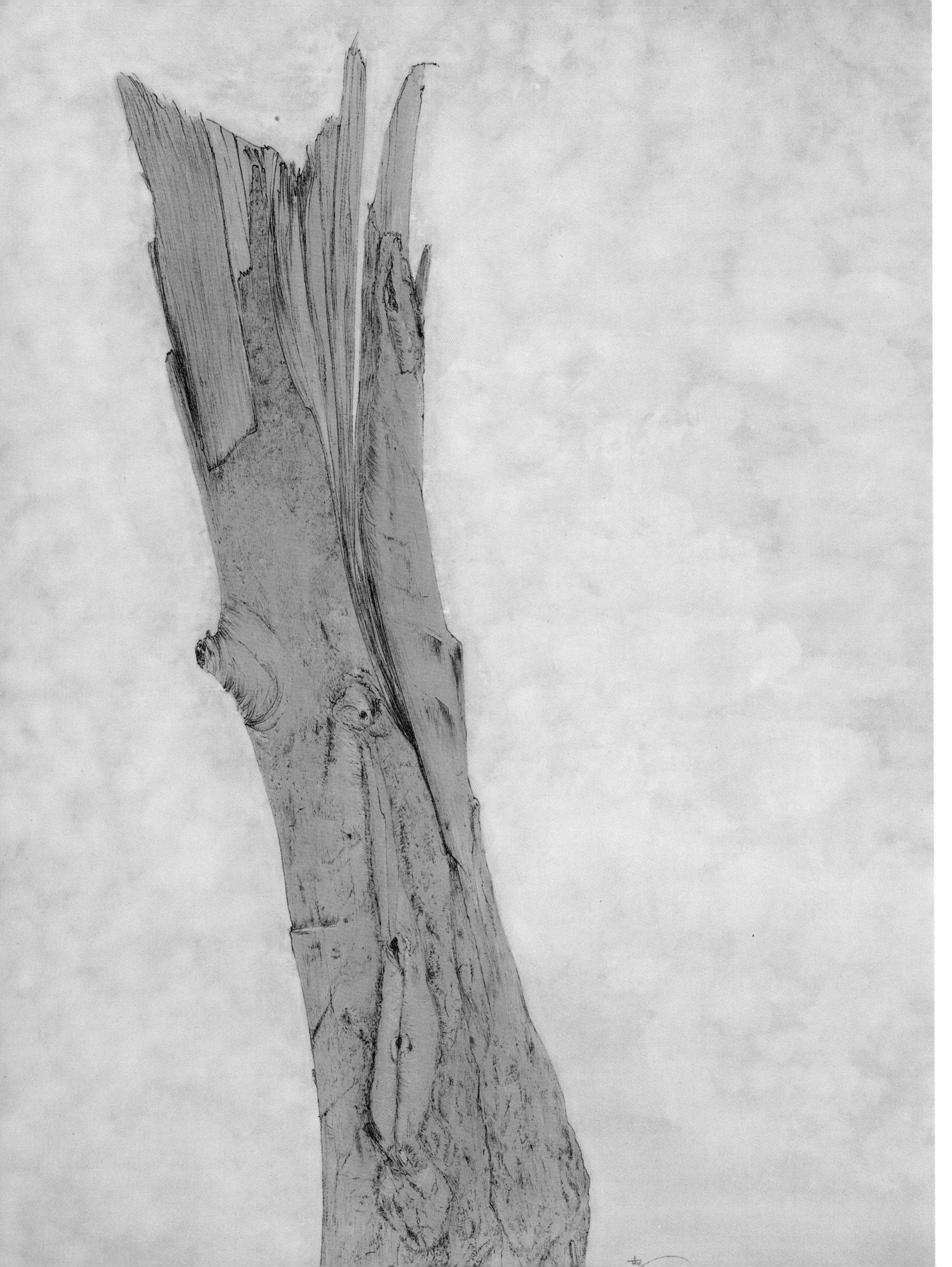

Splintered Log
Yaddo, New York, 1961
watercolor and pen and india ink on paper
25 5/8 x 19 5/8 inches

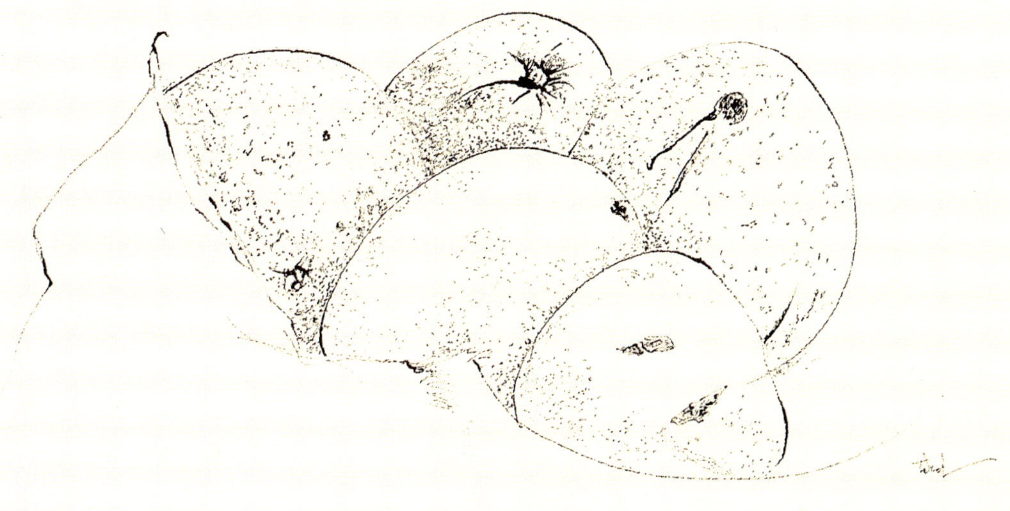

Oranges
Spain, 1961
pen and india ink on paper
11 1/4 x 17 1/2 inches

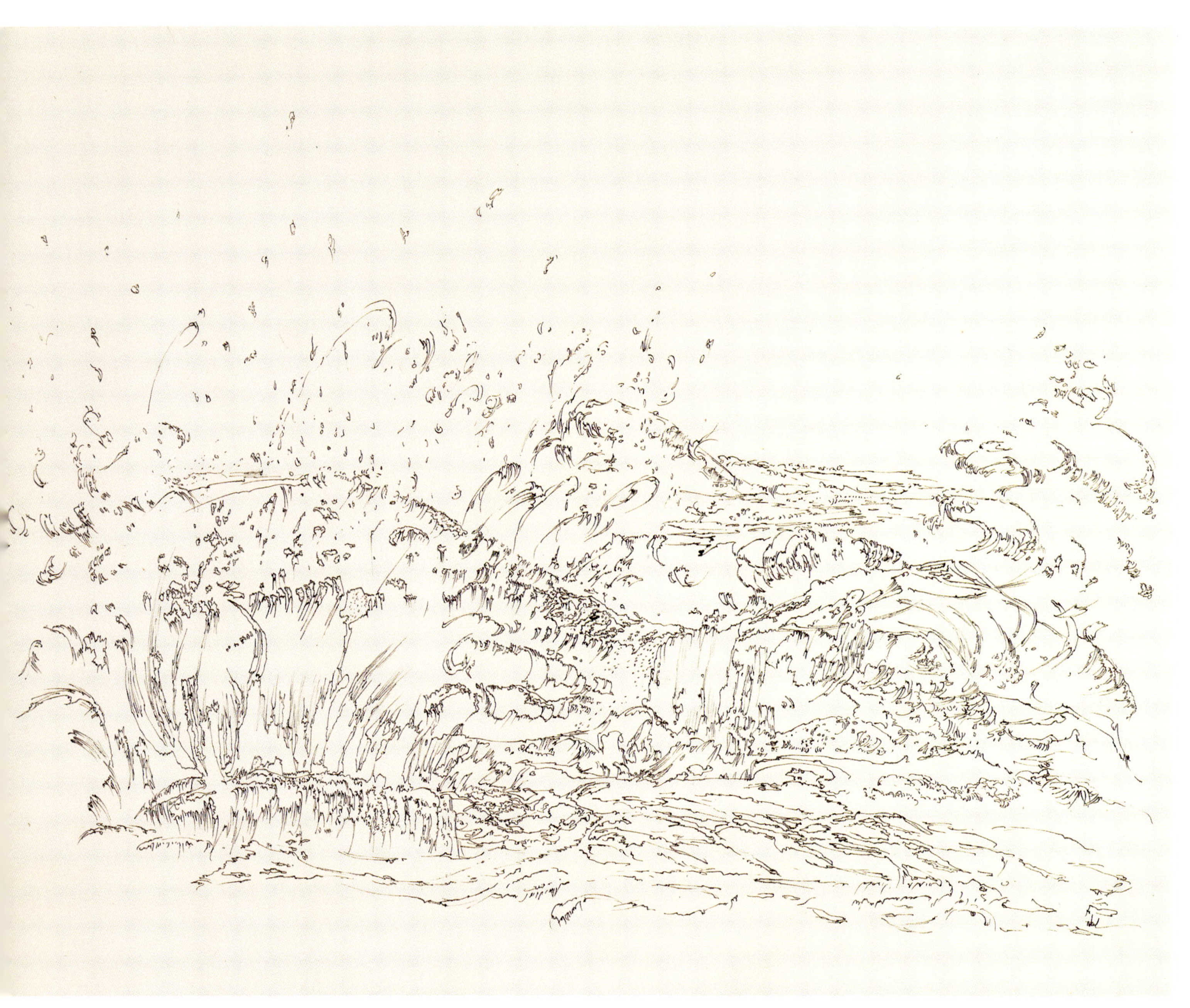

Surf
Long Island, New York, 1962
pen and india ink on paper
18 7/8 x 24 inches

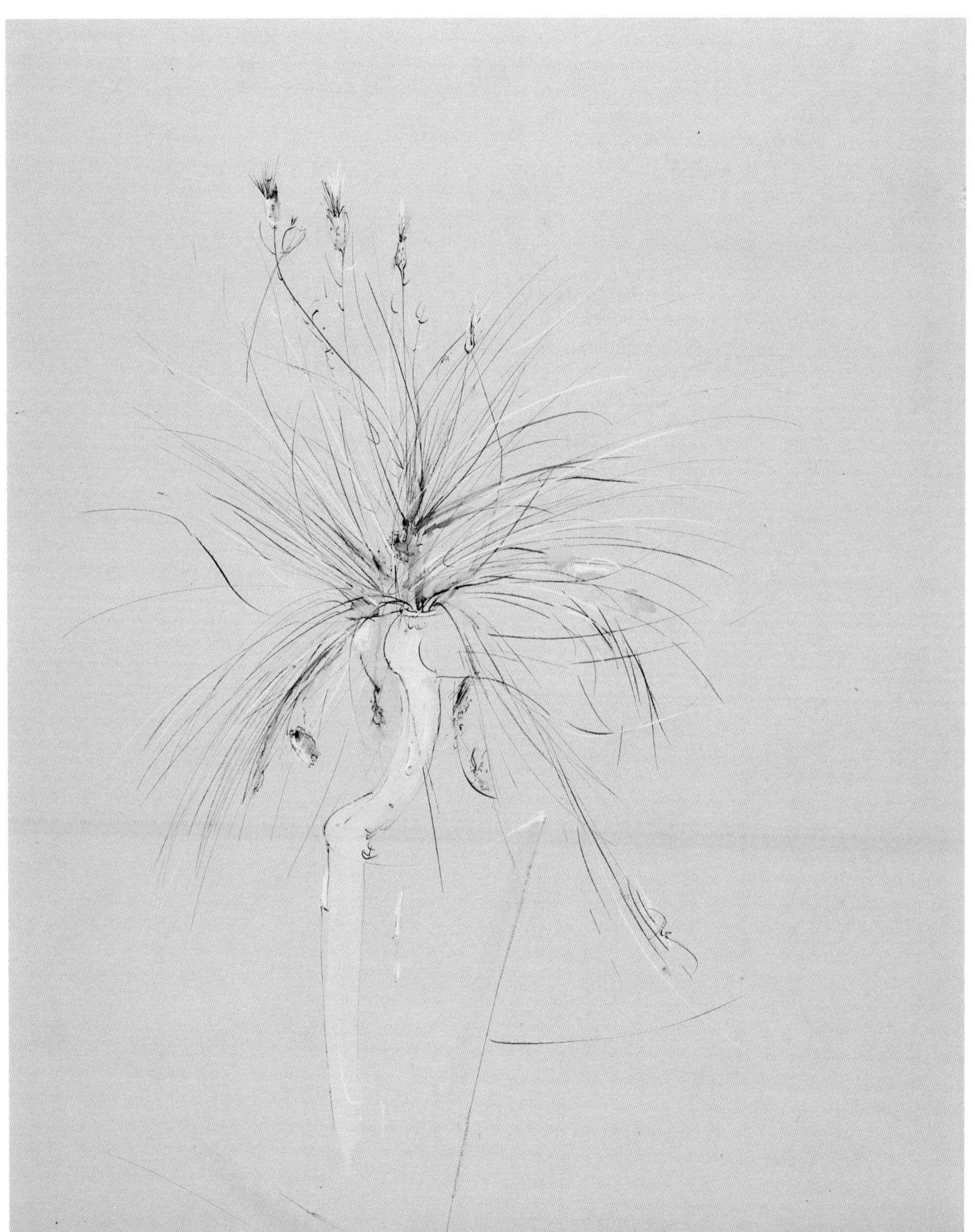

Grasses in Bottle
Saylorsburg, Pennsylvania, 1962
pen and india ink with light yellow and brown accents on gray paper
26 1/4 x 20 1/8 inches

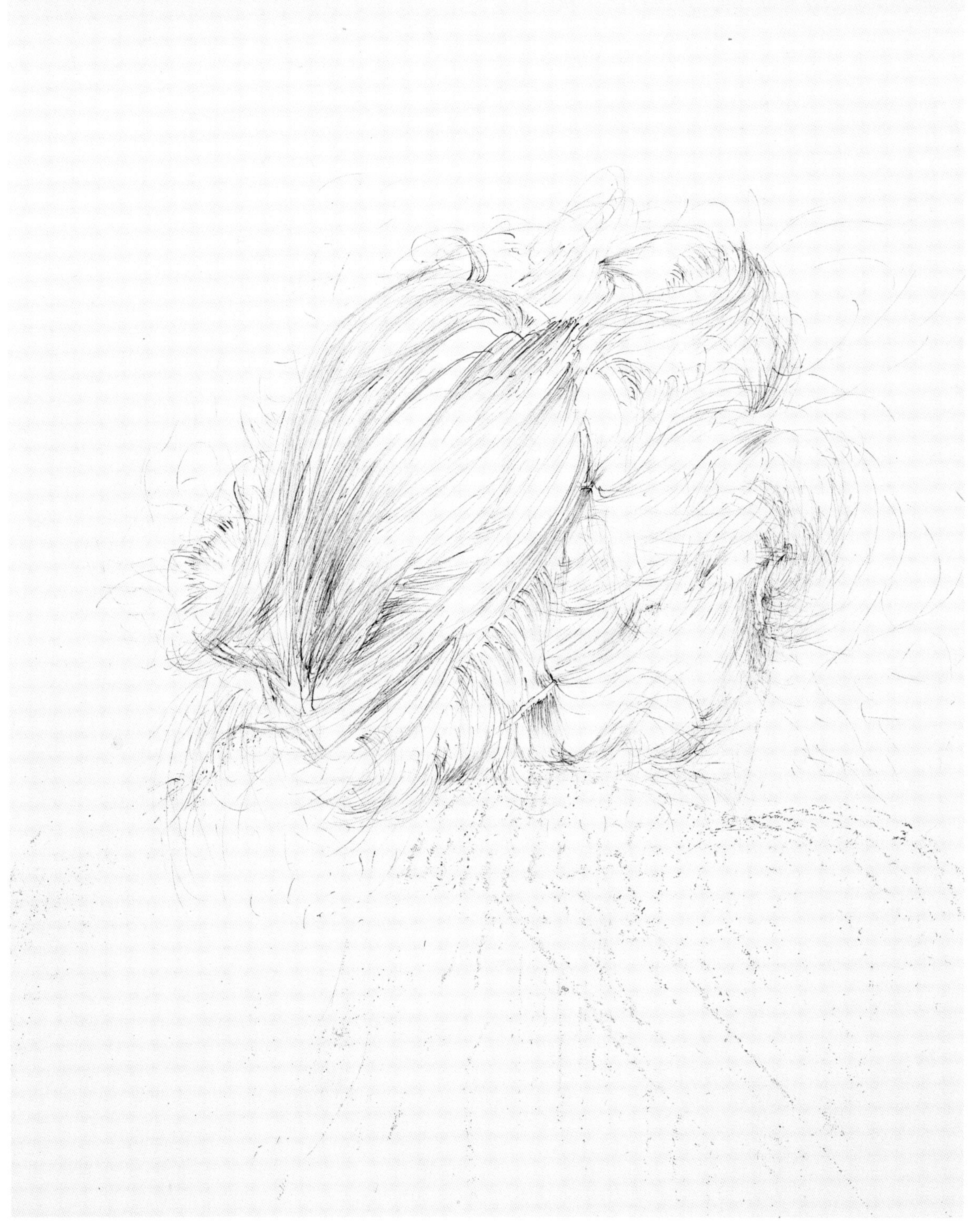

Back of a Woman's Head
Saylorsburg, Pennsylvania, 1963
pen and india ink on paper
20 3/8 x 20 5/8 inches

Day Dreamer
Saylorsburg, Pennsylvania, 1963
pen and sepia ink on paper
18 5/8 x 27 1/8 inches

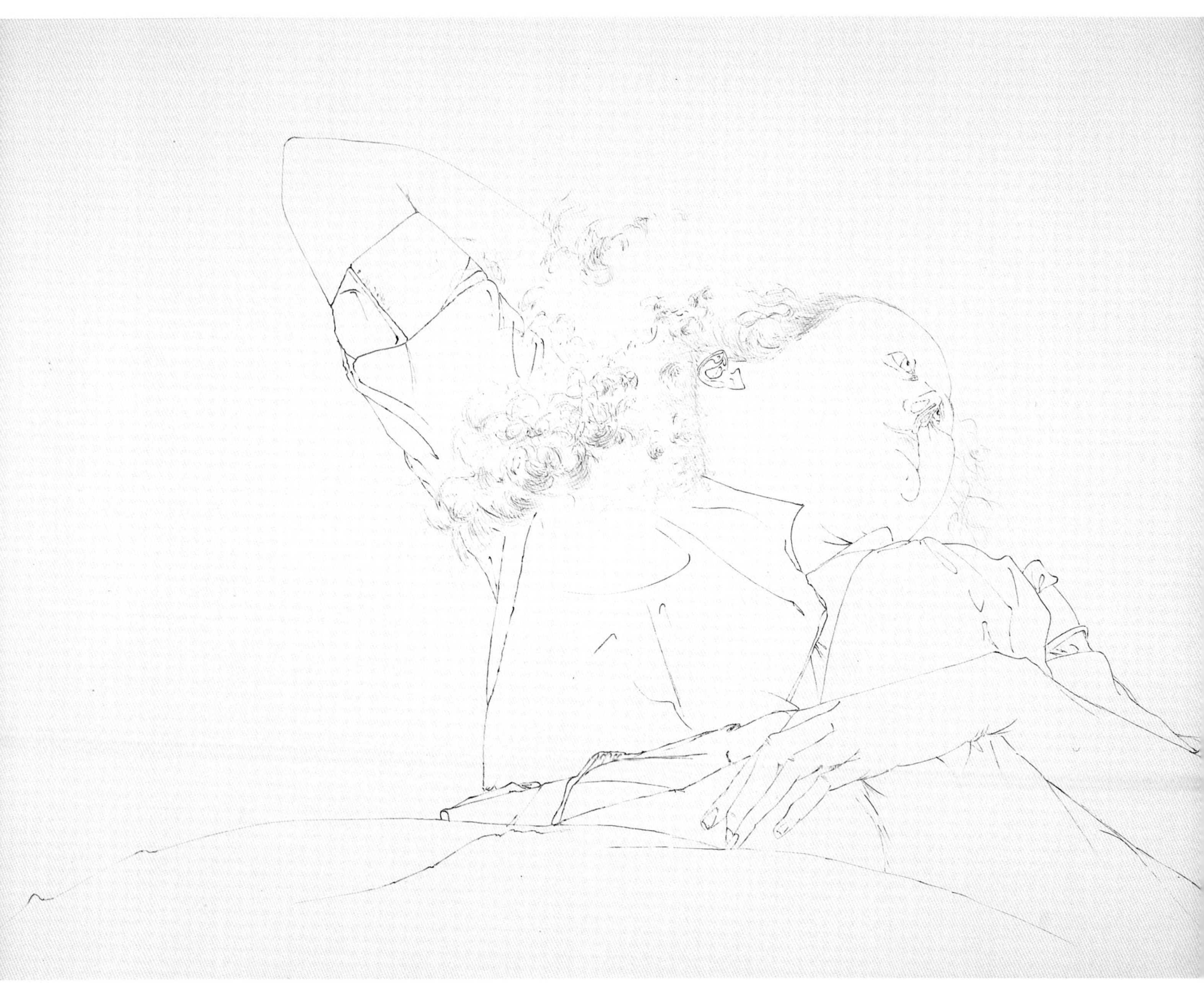

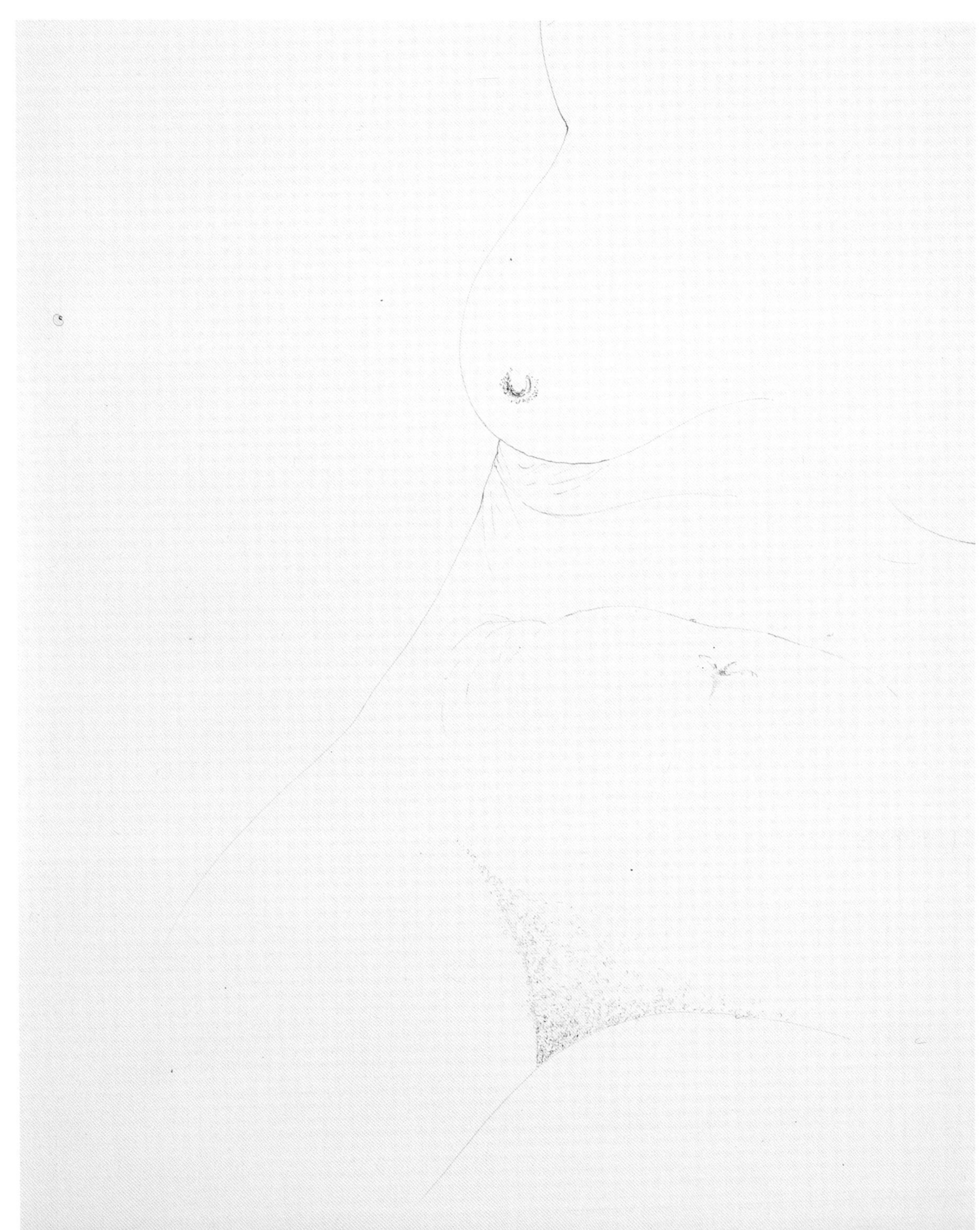

Nude (As Landscape)
Saylorsburg, Pennsylvania, 1963
pen and sepia ink on paper
16 3/4 x 13 5/8 inches

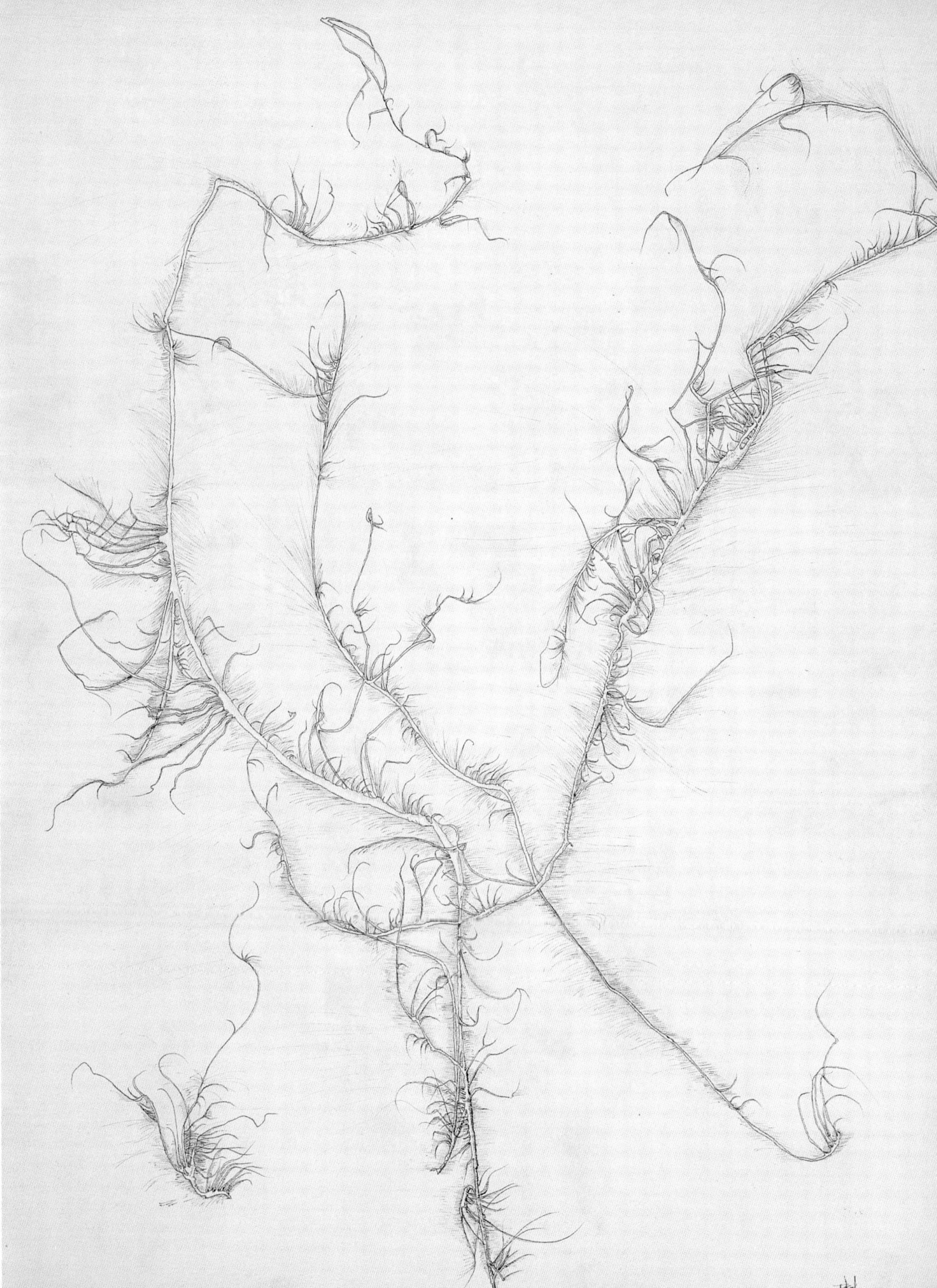

Roots
Saylorsburg, Pennsylvania, 1963
en and india ink and light orange wash on paper
30 1/2 x 22 1/2 inches

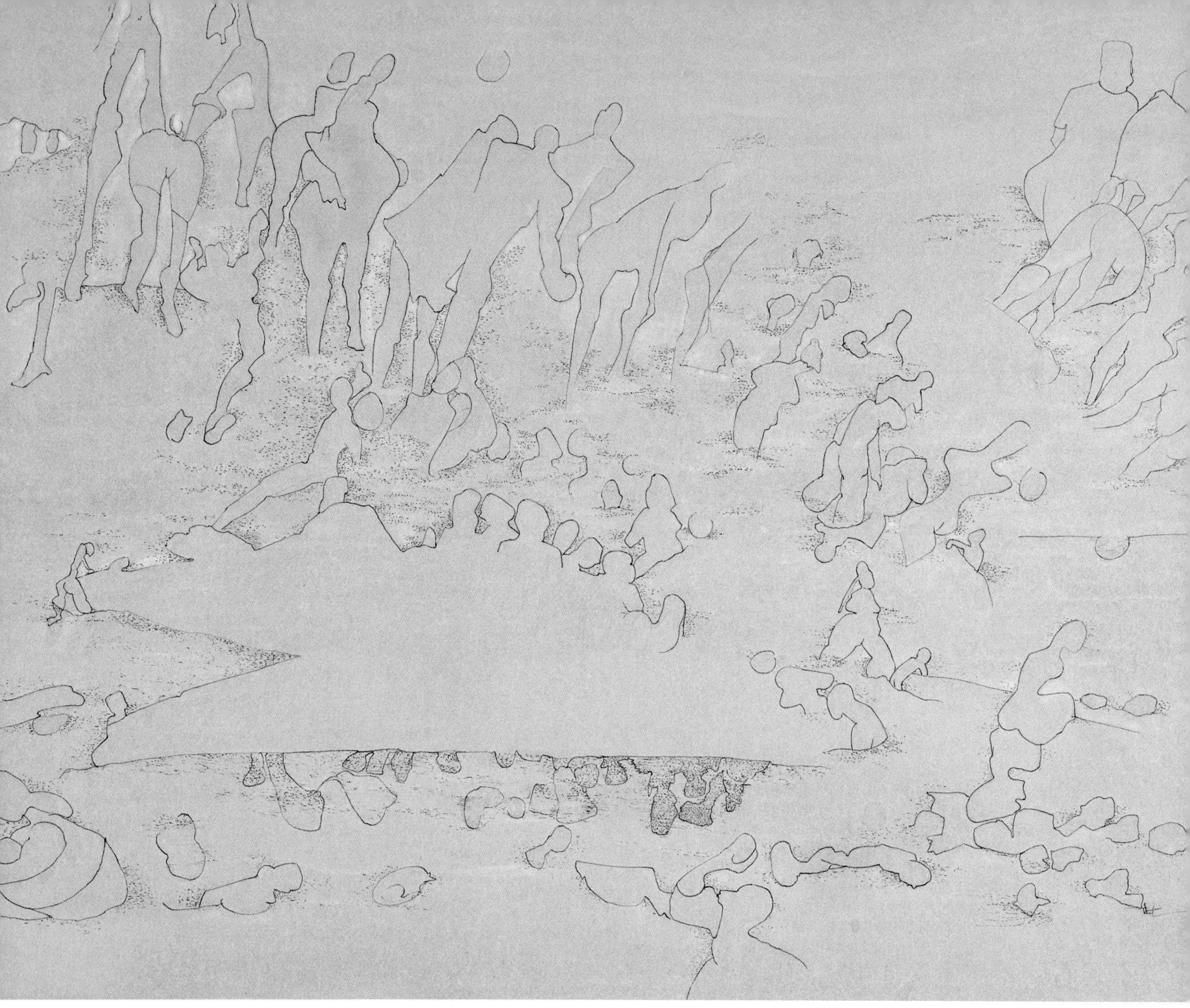

People on the Beach
Saylorsburg, Pennsylvania, 1965
pen and sepia ink and wash on paper
19 1/8 x 24 1/4 inches

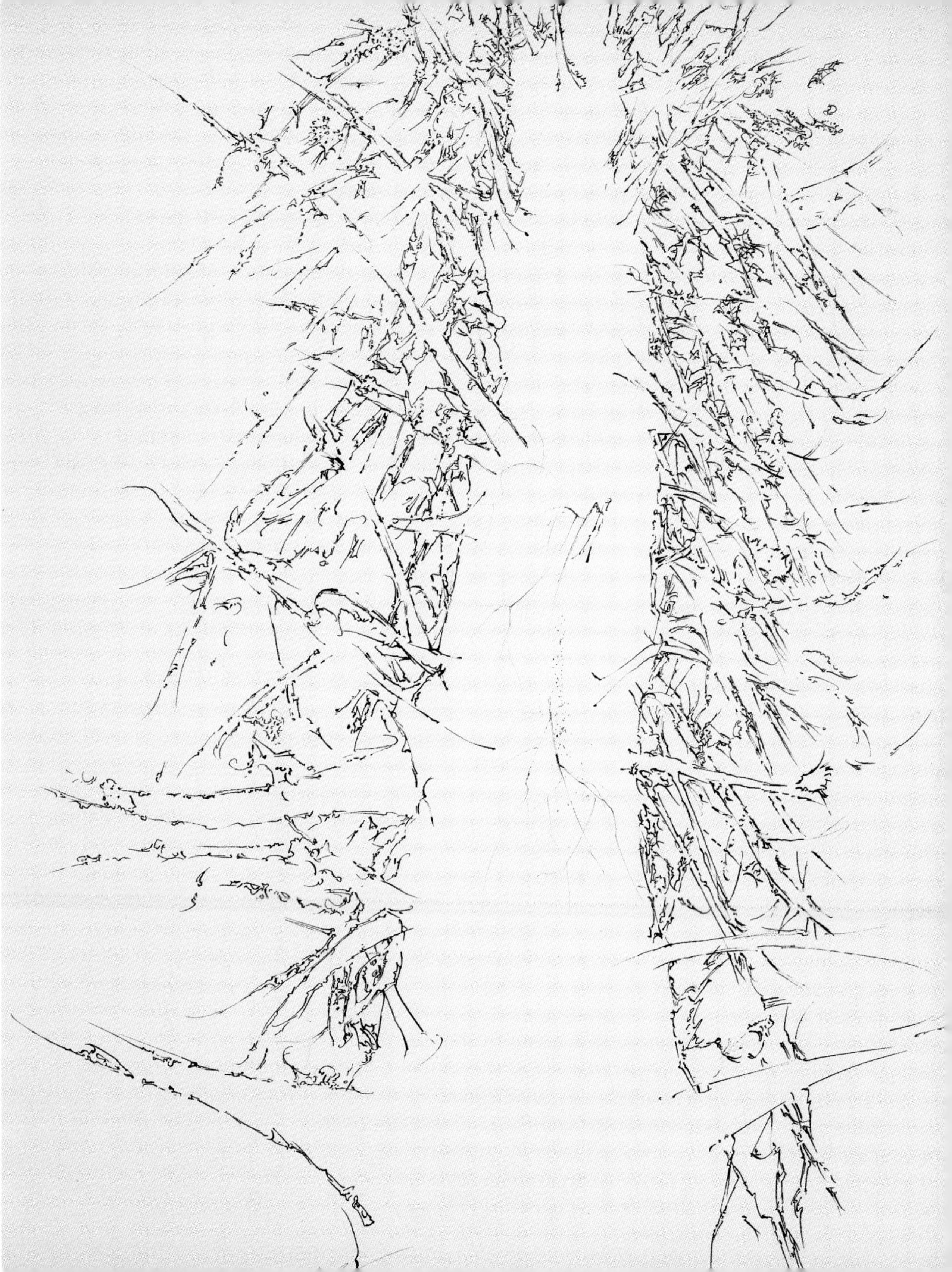

69

Clouds
Saylorsburg, Pennsylvania, 1966
pen and india ink on paper
22 5/8 x 28 1/2 inches

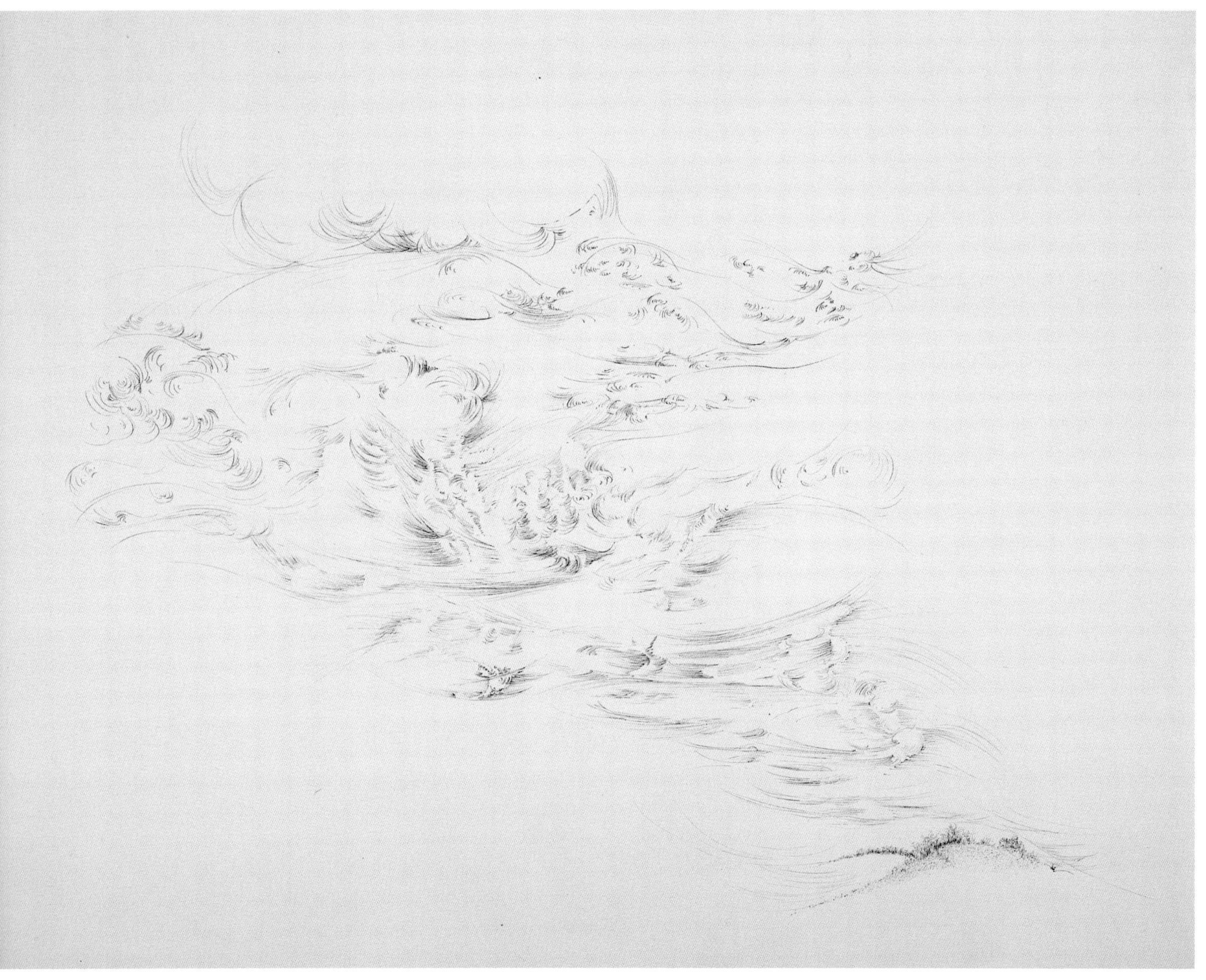

Root
Saylorsburg, Pennsylvania, 1966
silverpoint on prepared paper
20 x 23 7/8 inches

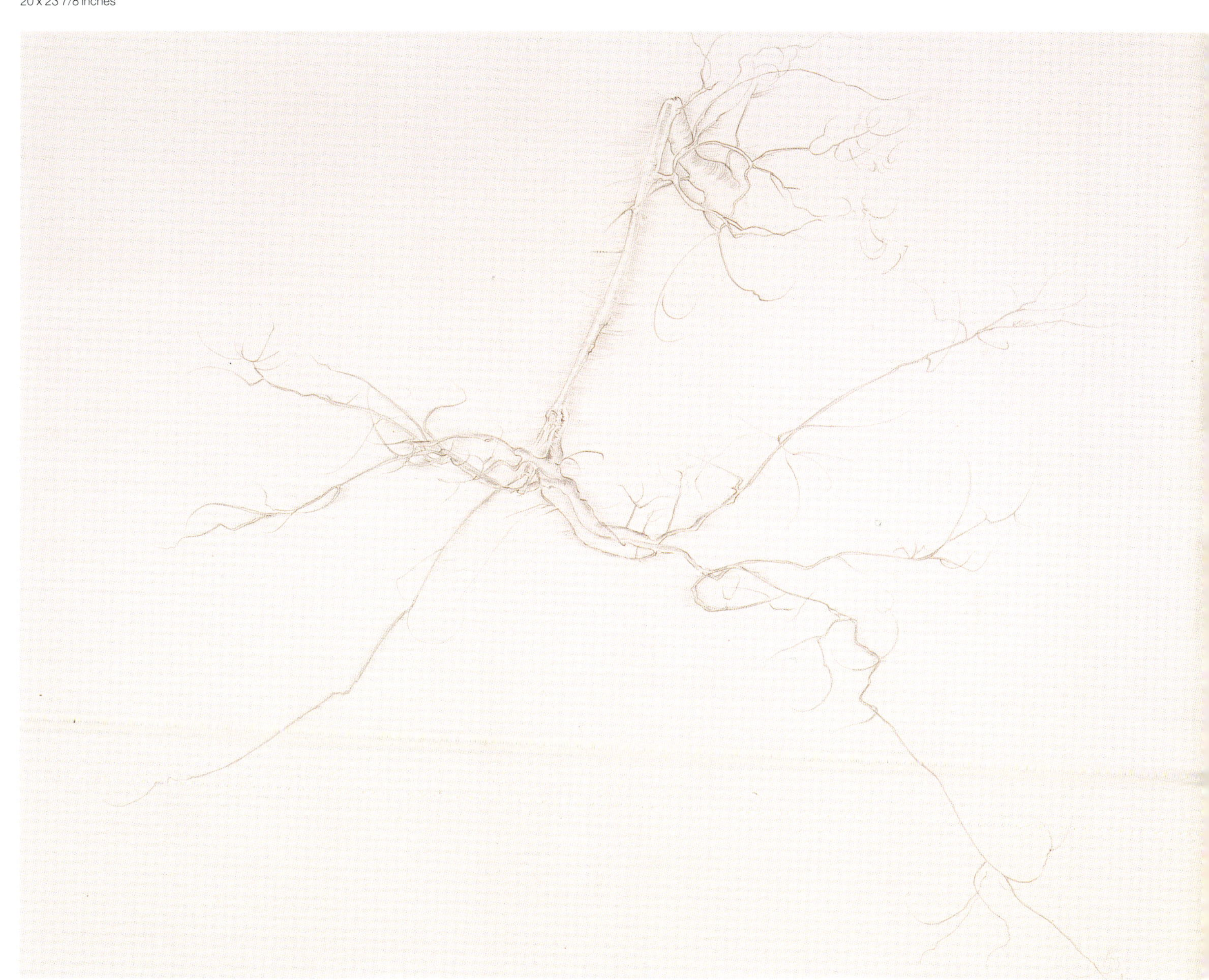

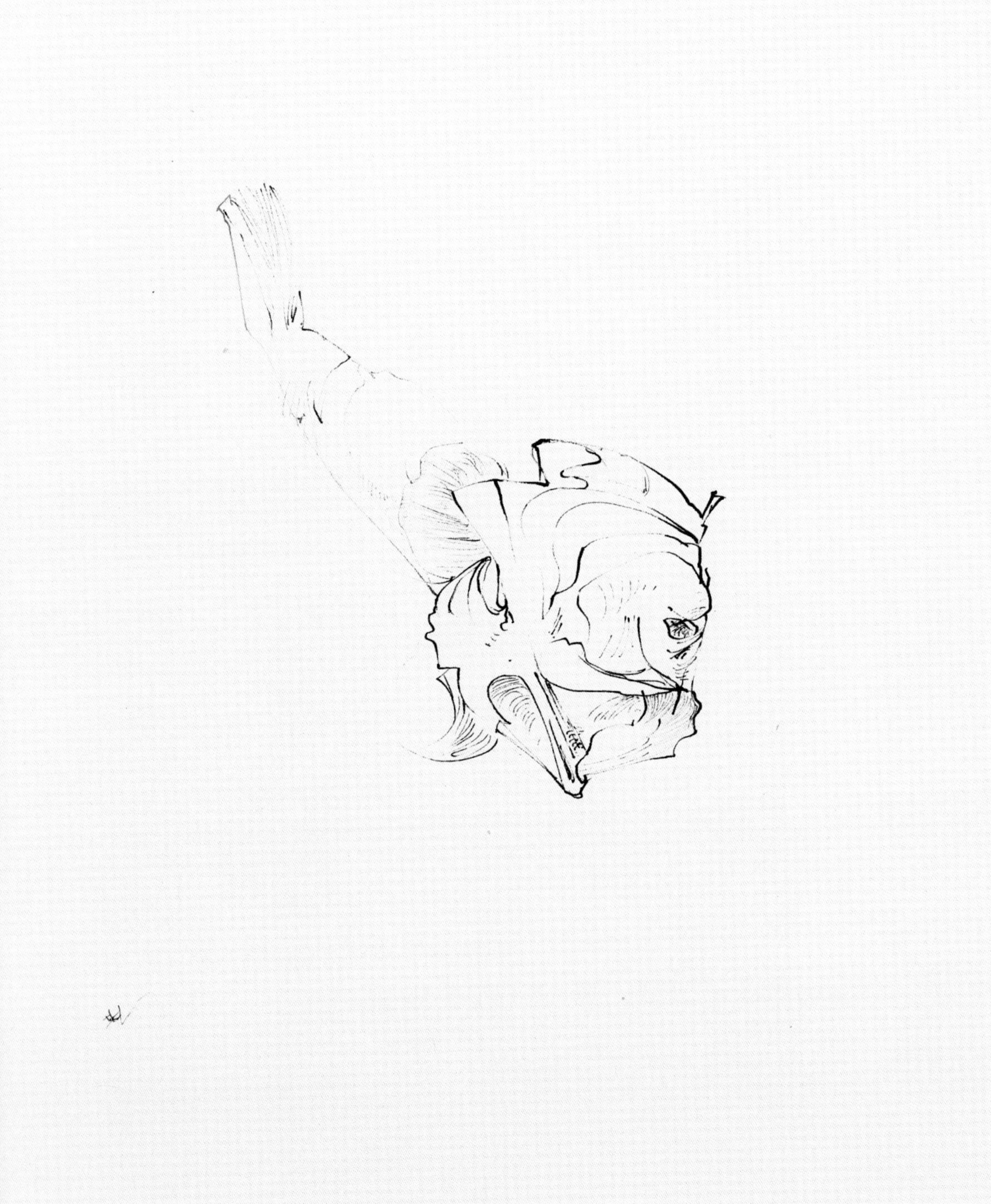

Bloater
Saylorsburg, Pennsylvania, 1967
pen and india ink on paper
14 x 10 3/4 inches

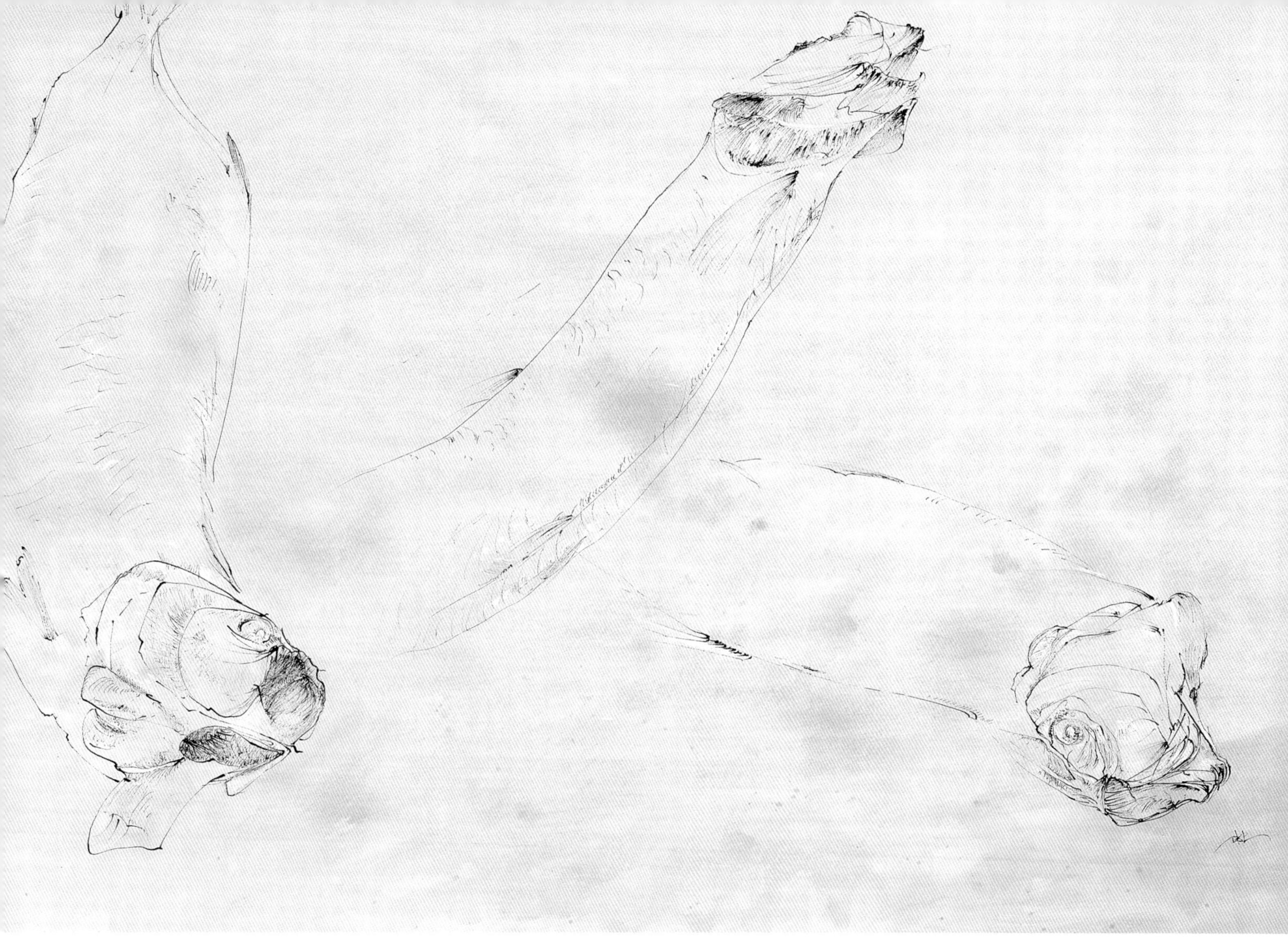

Three Fishes
Saylorsburg, Pennsylvania, 1967
pen and sepia ink and orange wash on paper
18 3/8 x 27 1/2 inches

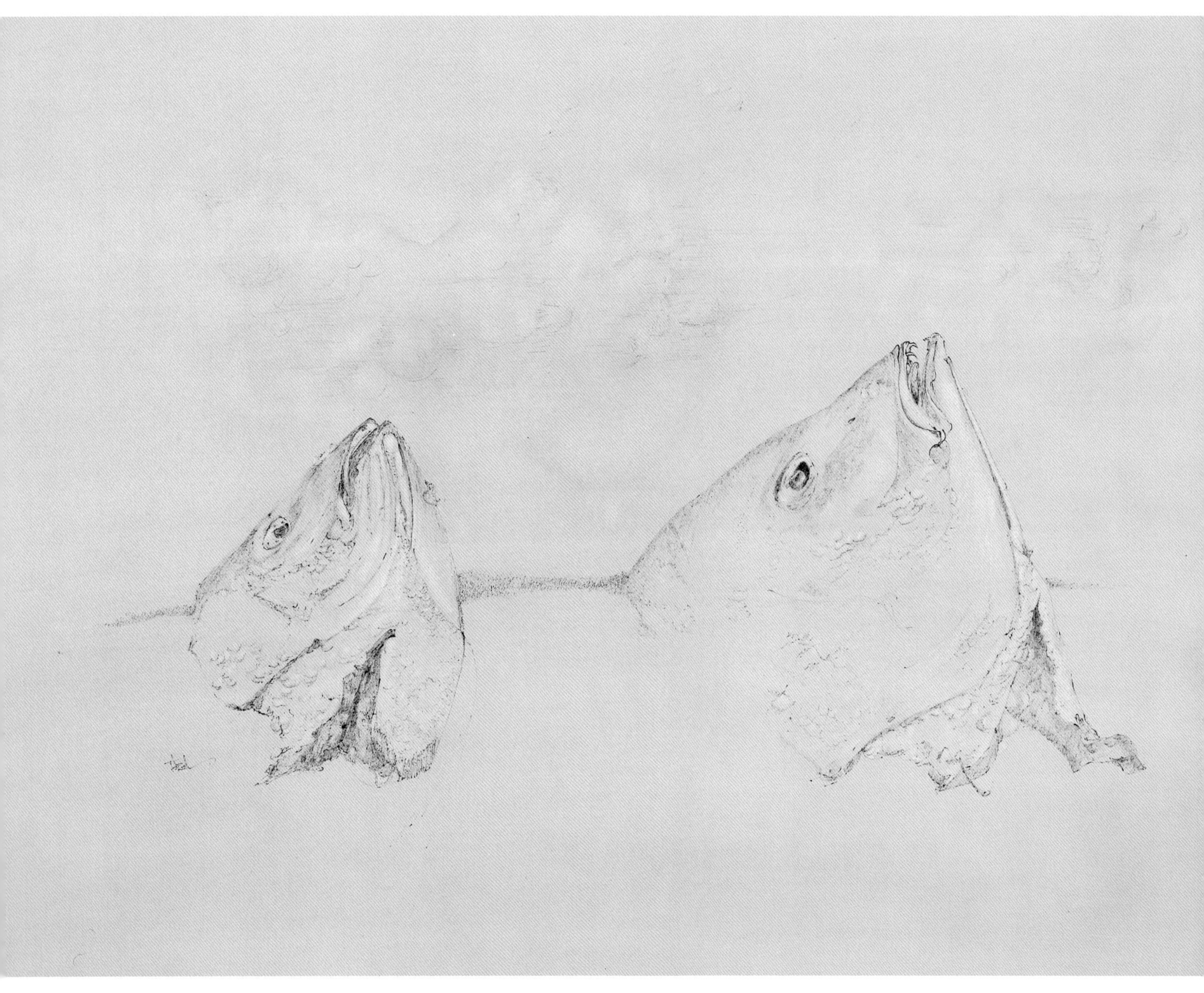

Fish Heads
Maine, 1967
pen and sepia ink and orange wash on paper
20 5/8 x 25 7/8 inches

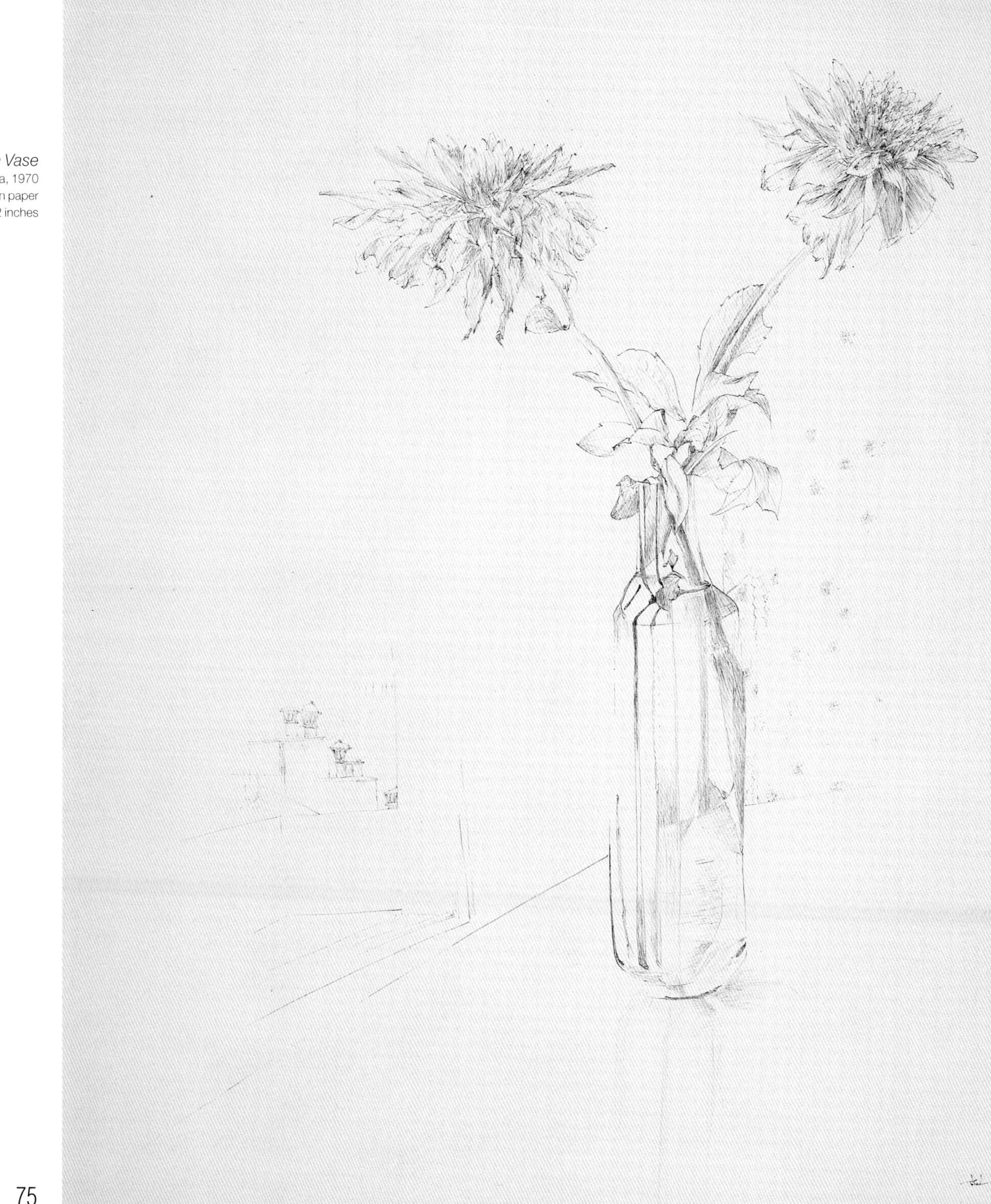

Dahlias in Vase
Geneva, 1970
pen and india ink on paper
30 x 22 1/2 inches

Slope
Geneva, 1971
pen and india ink and sepia ink on paper
25 5/8 x 20 3/8 inches

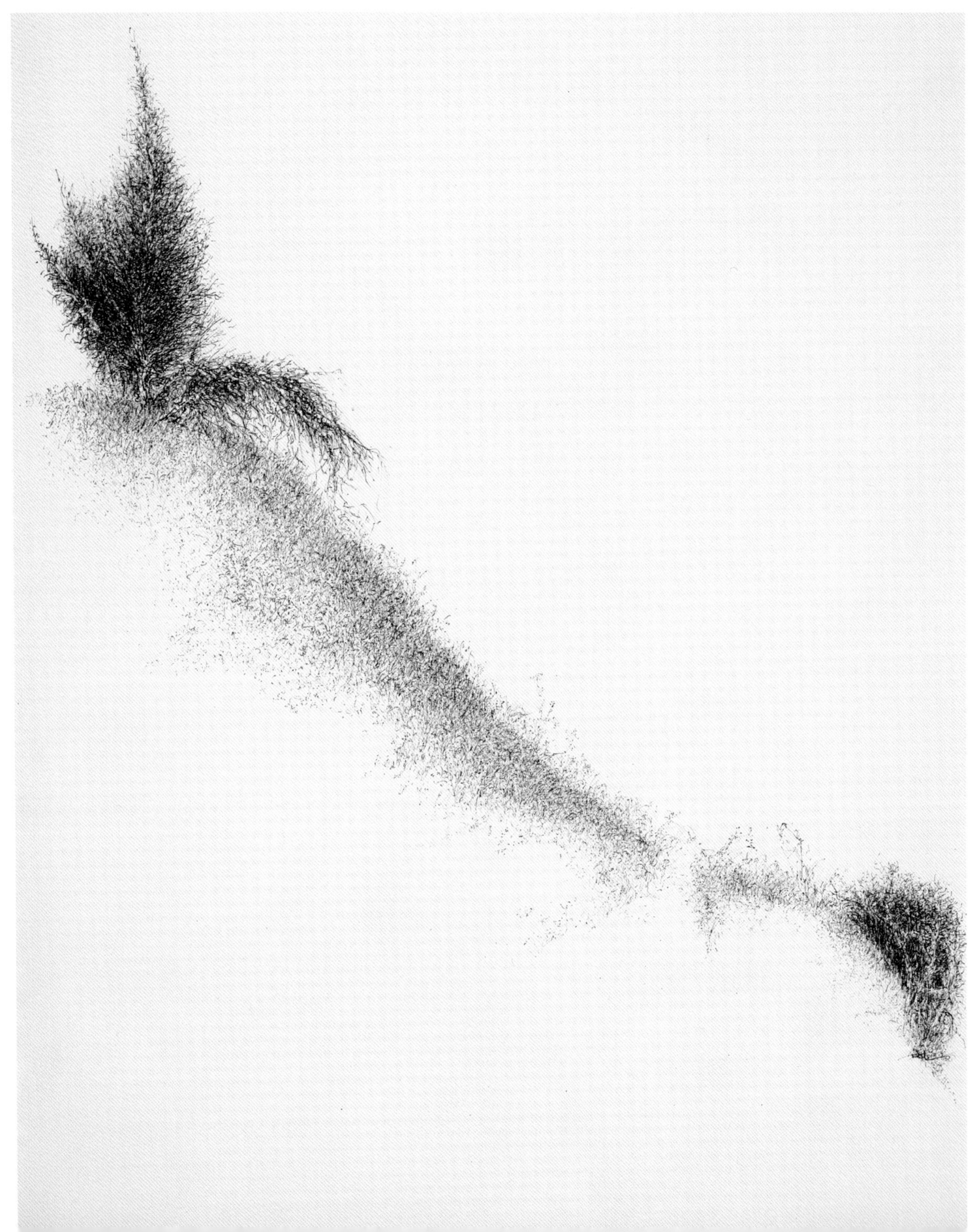

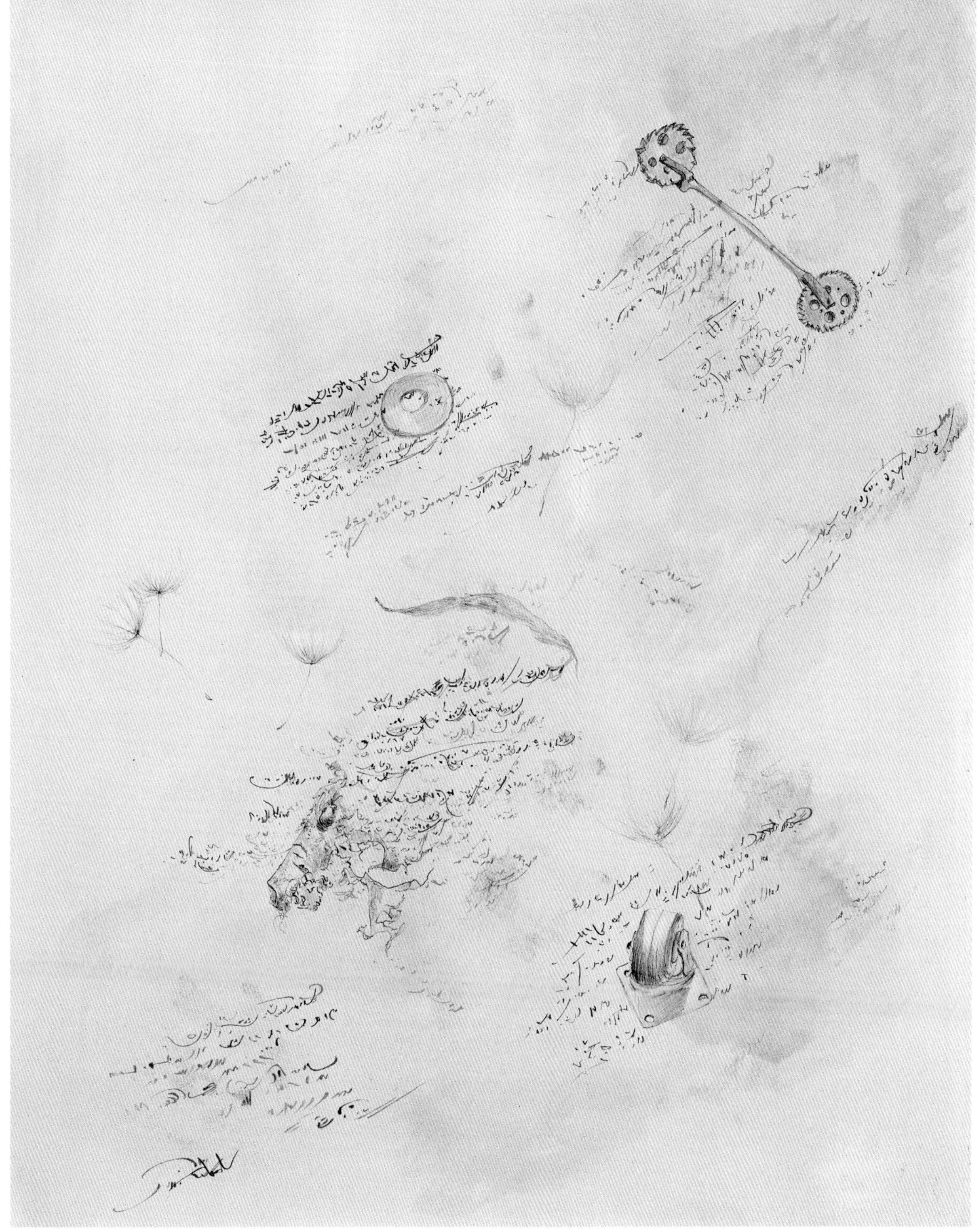

Blotter Gossip
Geneva, 1973
pen and color ink and wash on paper
25 5/8 x 20 3/4 inches

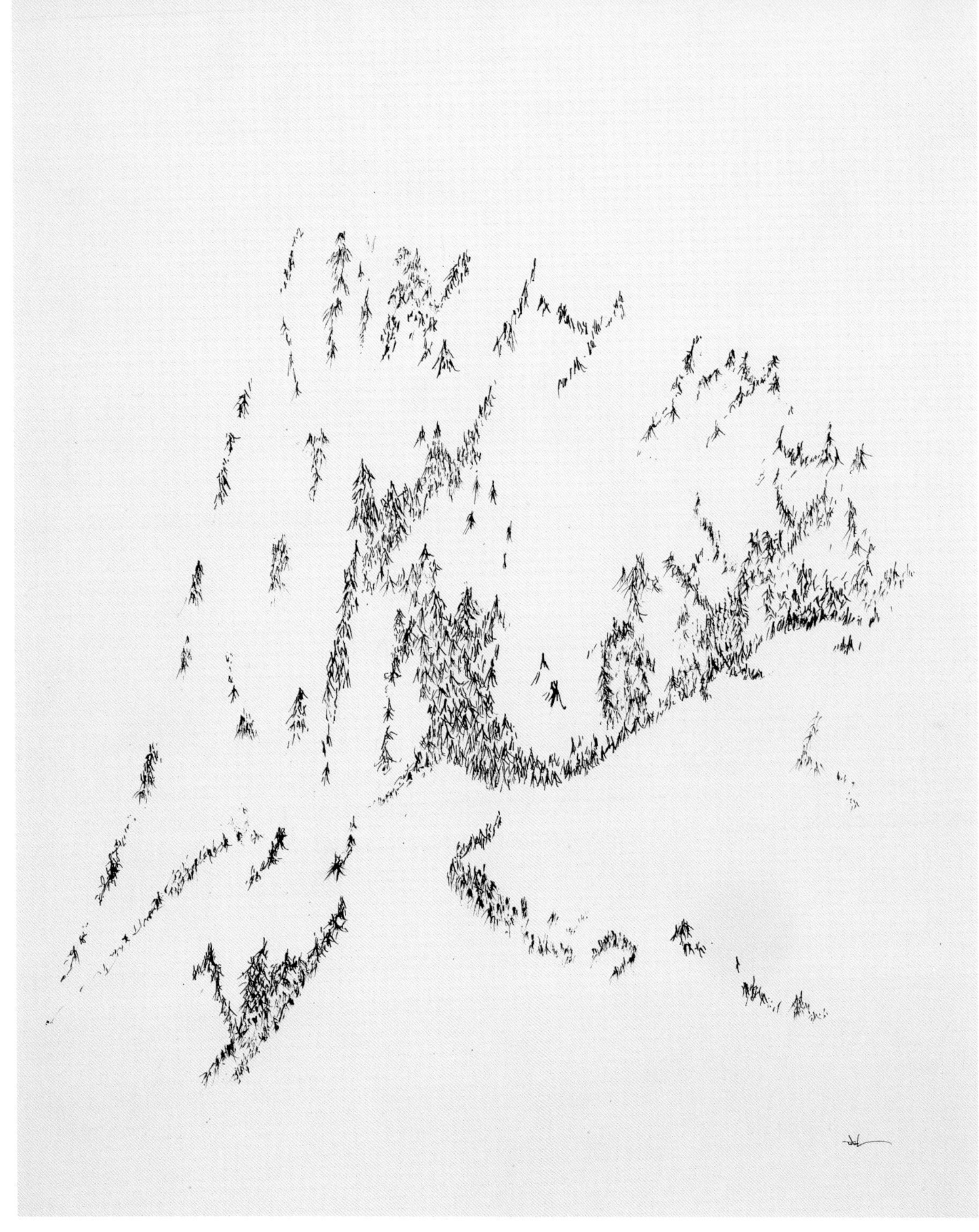

Snowy Mountainside
Savoie, France, 1973
pen and india ink on paper
25 5/8 x 20 7/8 inches

Phoenix
Geneva, 1975
pen and india ink on paper
28 3/8 x 20 5/8 inches

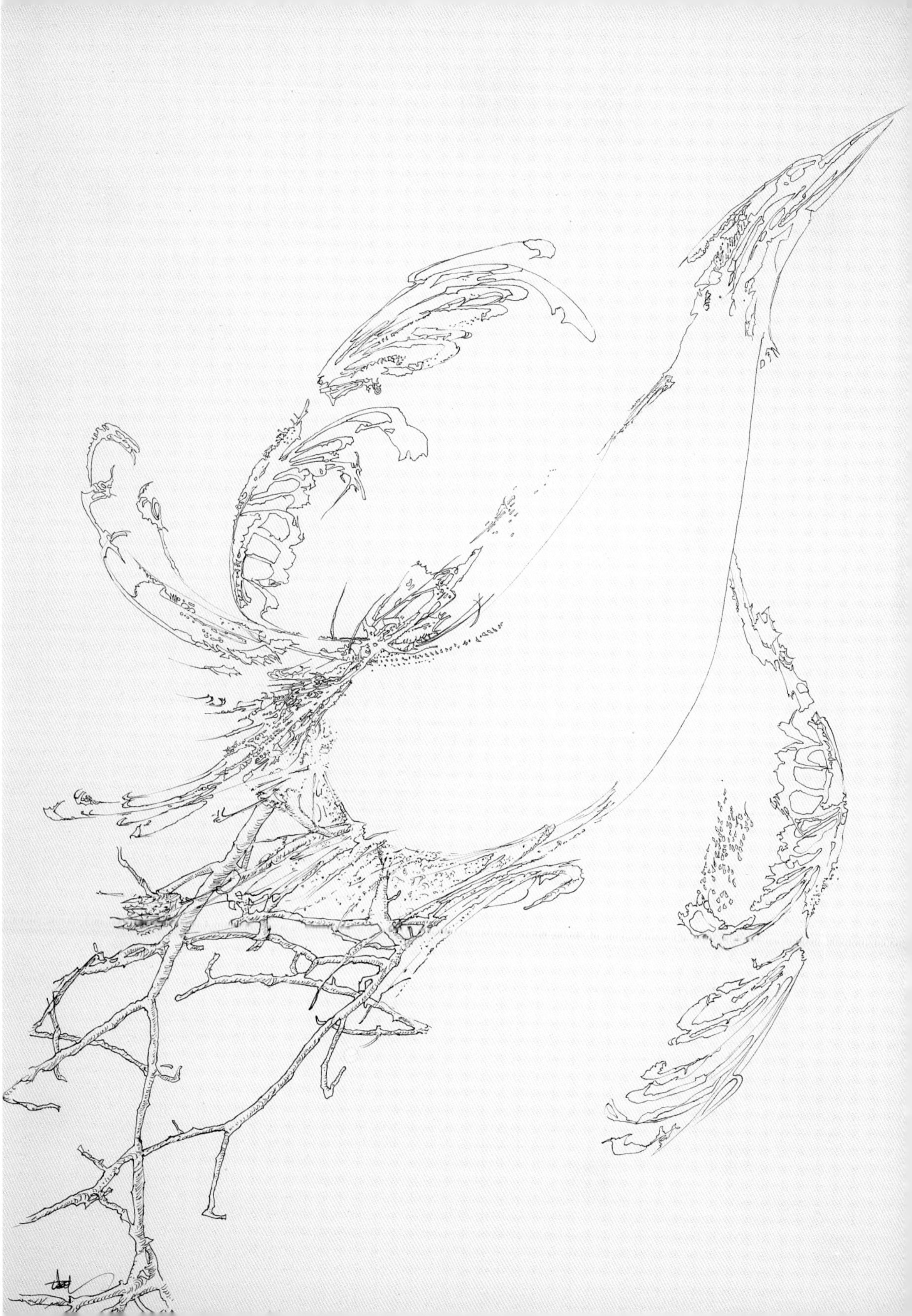

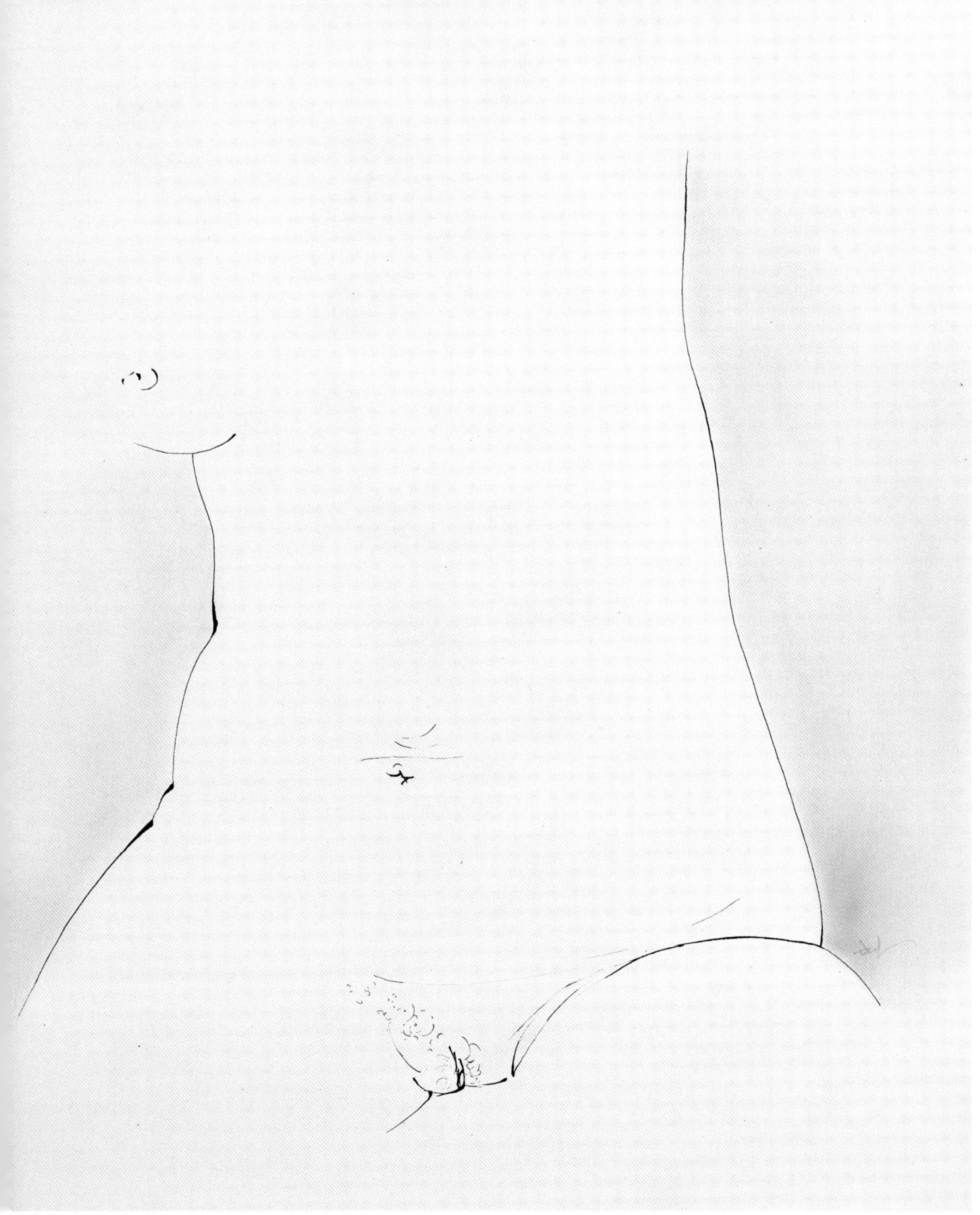

Torso
Geneva, 1975
pen and india ink with gray wash on paper
25 5/8 x 20 3/4 inches

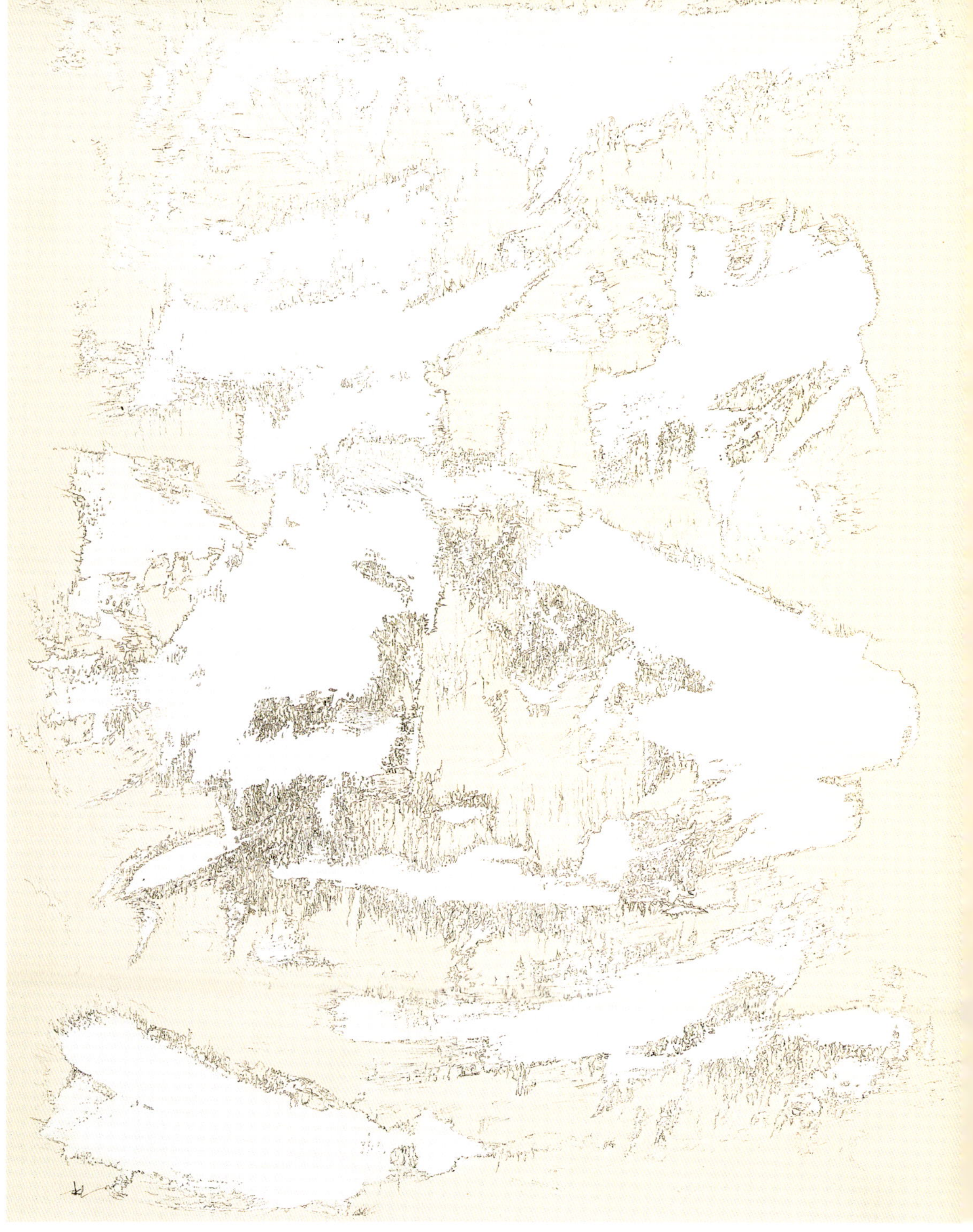

Winter Bark
Geneva, 1976
pen and india ink and white acrylic on paper
25 5/8 x 20 5/8 inches

Tree
Geneva, 1977
pen and sepia ink and wash on paper
20 5/8 x 25 9/16 inches

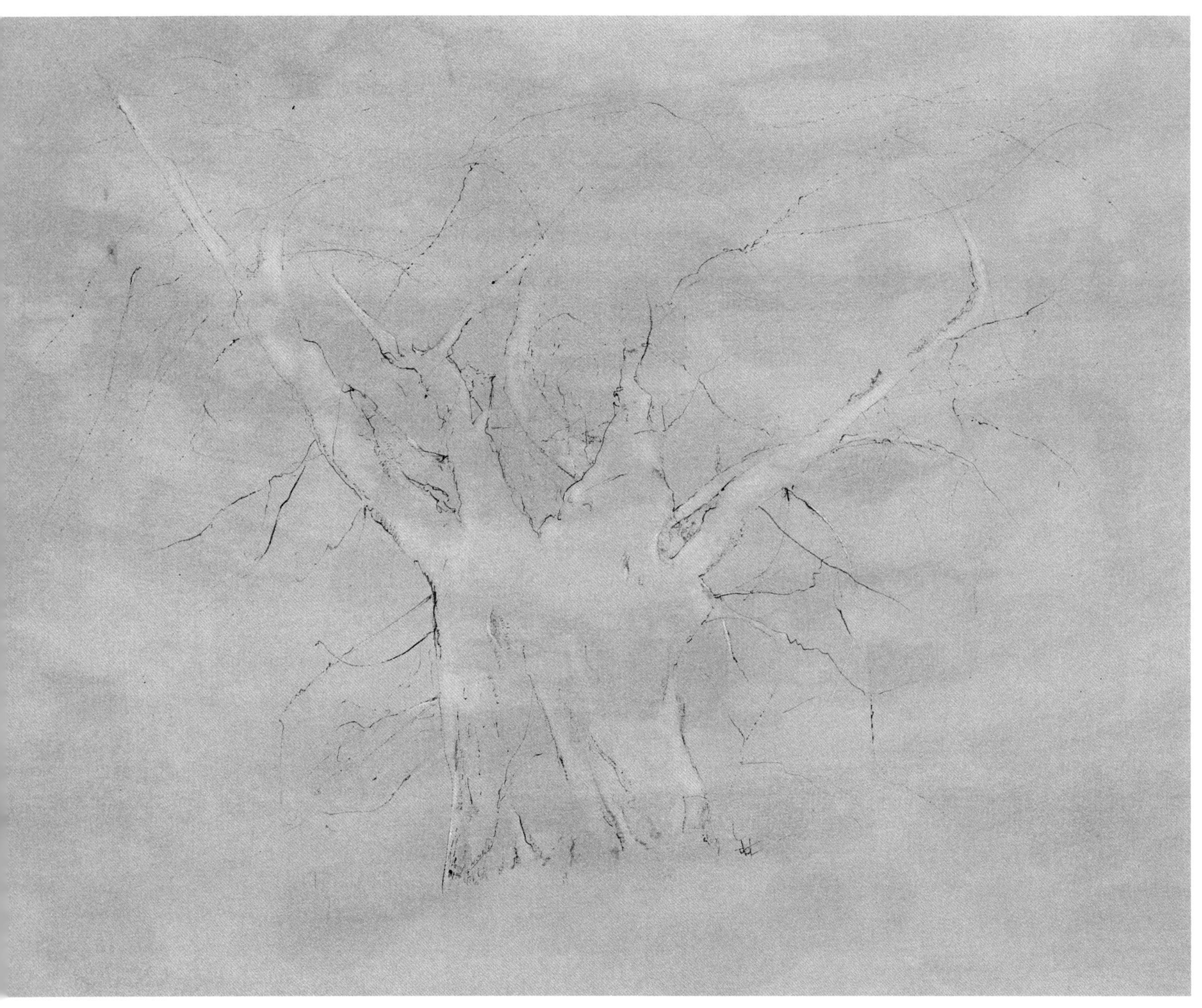

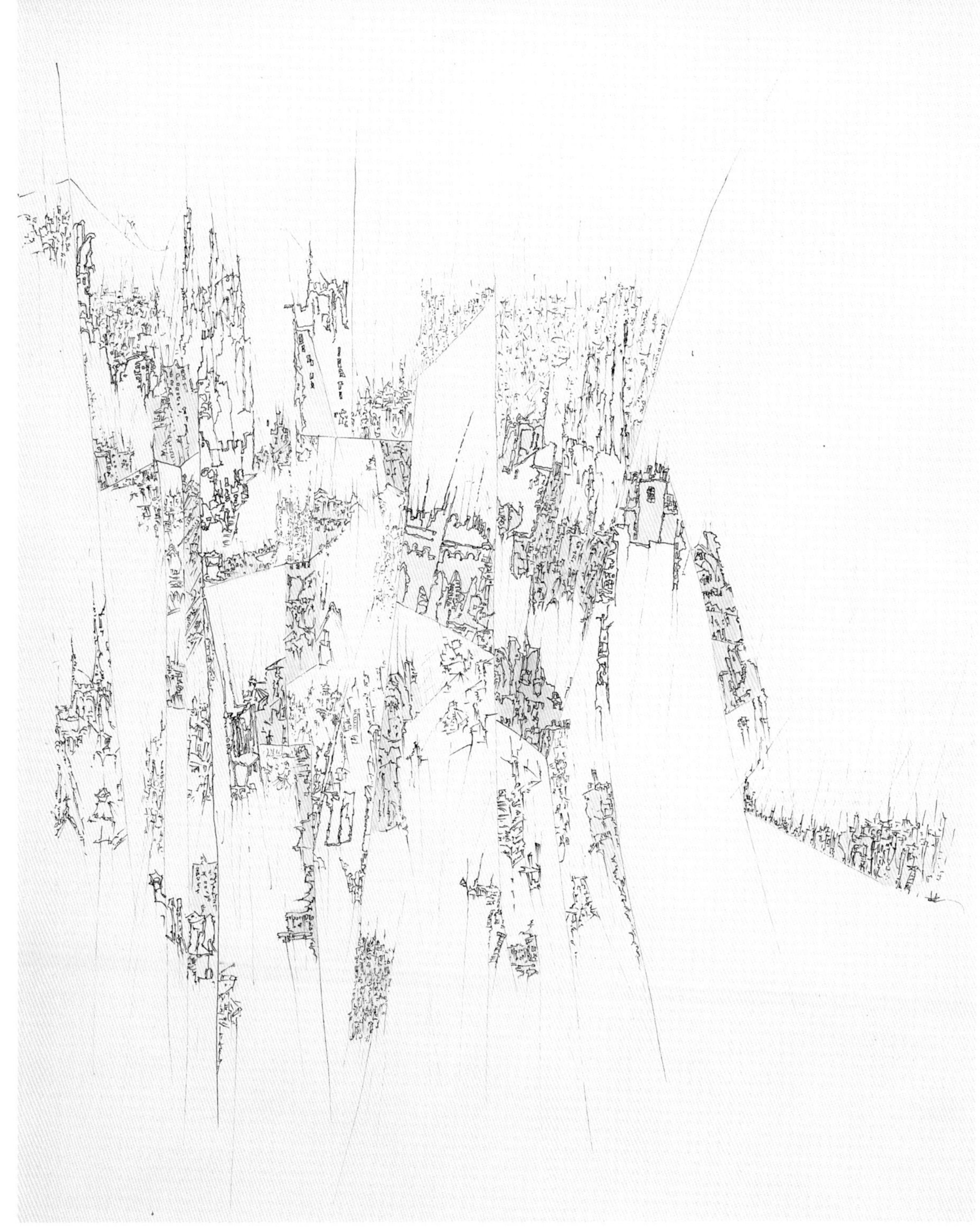

Cityscape
Geneva, 1977
pen and india ink and watercolor on paper
25 5/8 x 20 7/8 inches

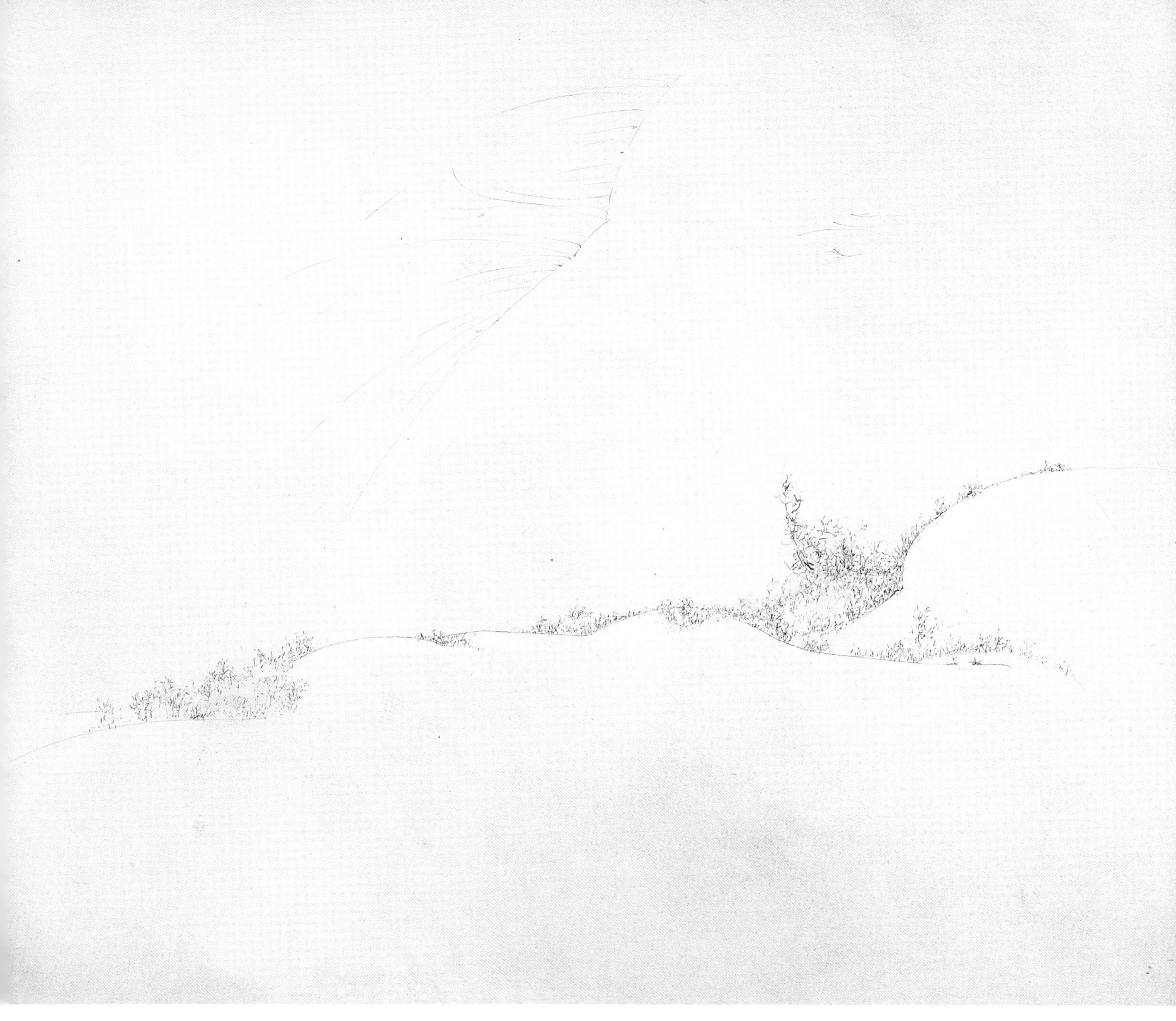

Landscape
Geneva, 1978
pen and sepia ink with gray accents on paper
20 3/4 x 25 5/8 inches

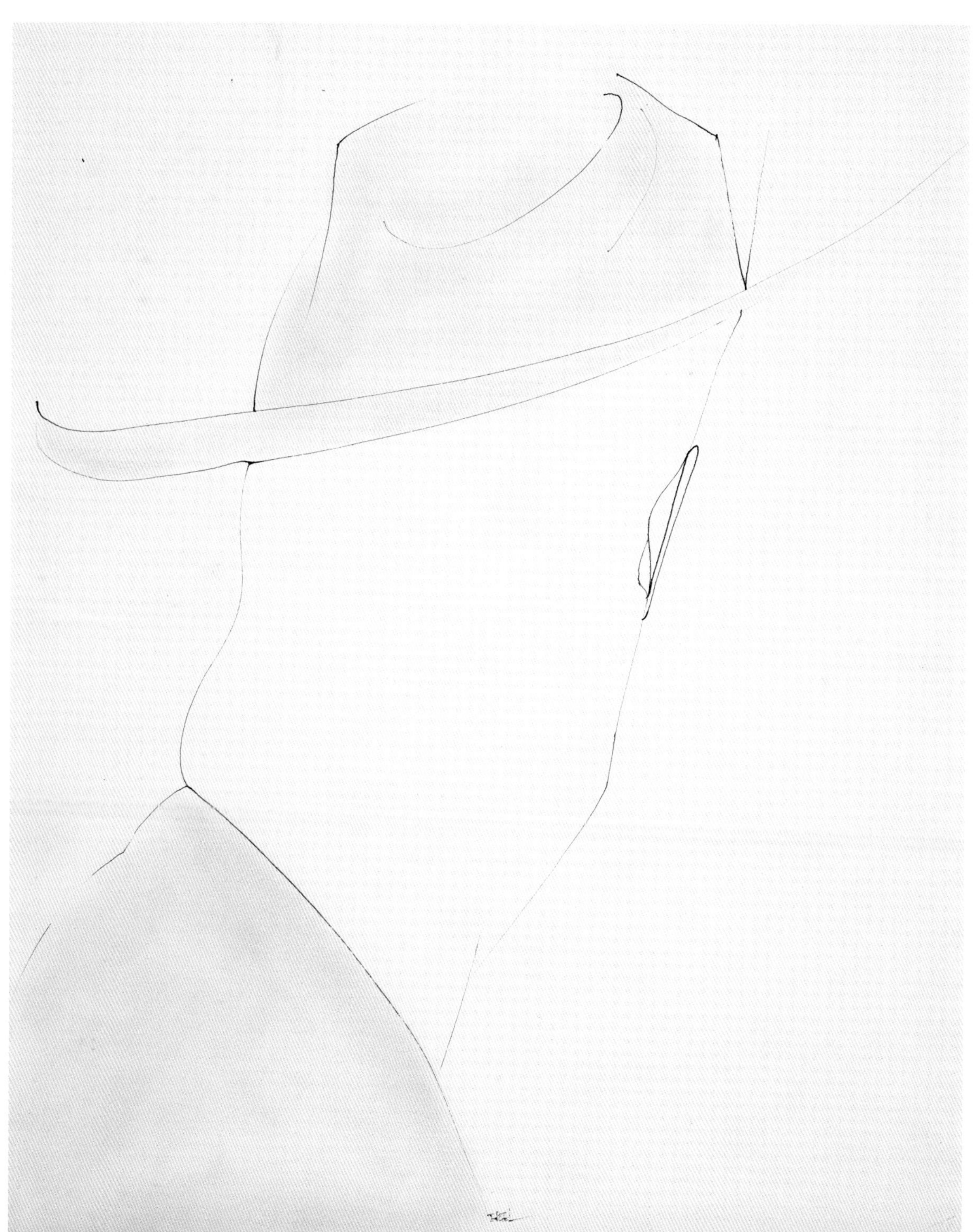

Man Wearing Hat
Saylorsburg, Pennsylvania, 1979
pen and india ink with gray accents on paper
26 x 20 5/8 inches

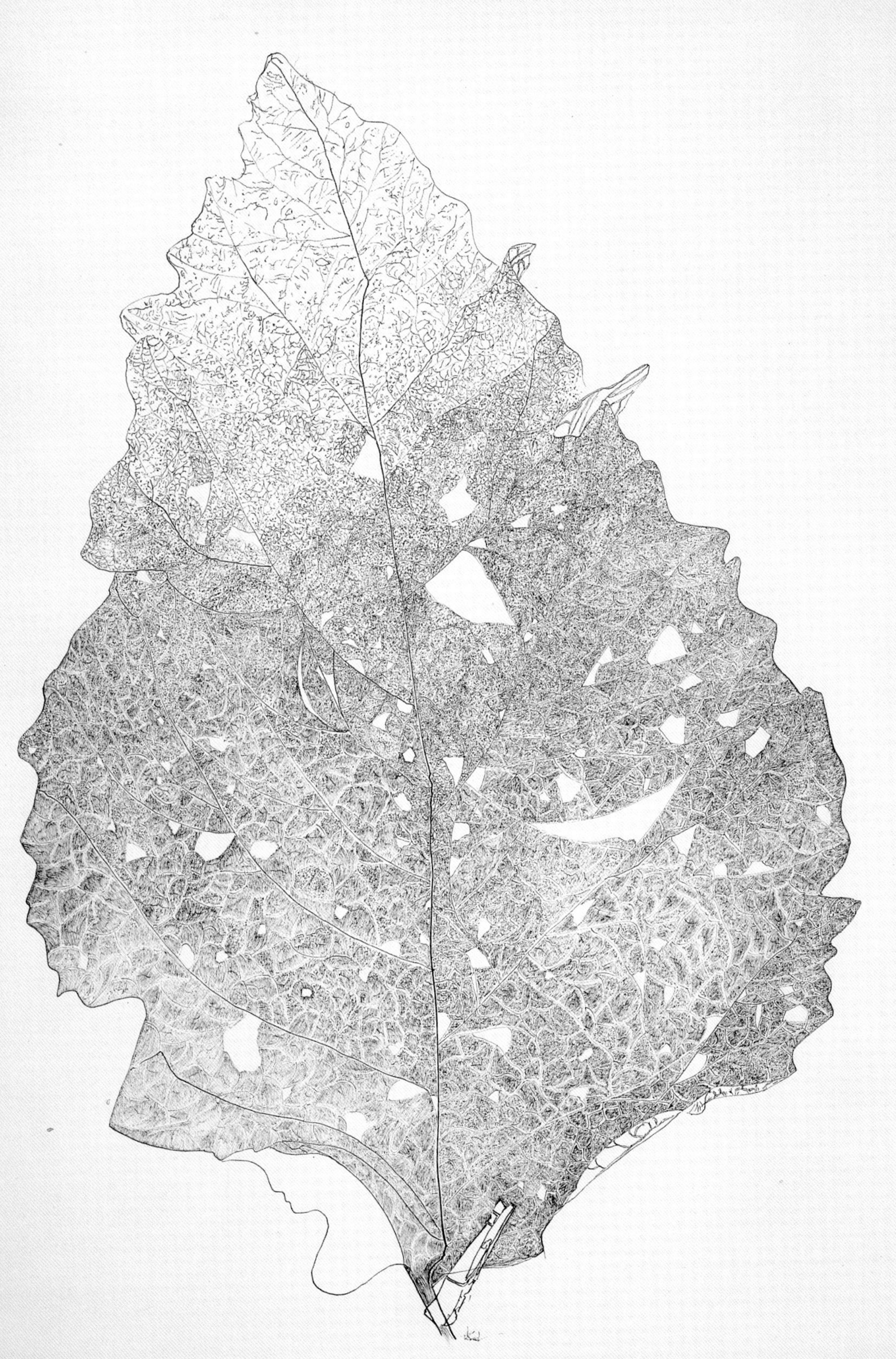

Leaf
Saylorsburg, Pennsylvania, 1982
pen and india ink on paper
30 x 22 1/4 inches

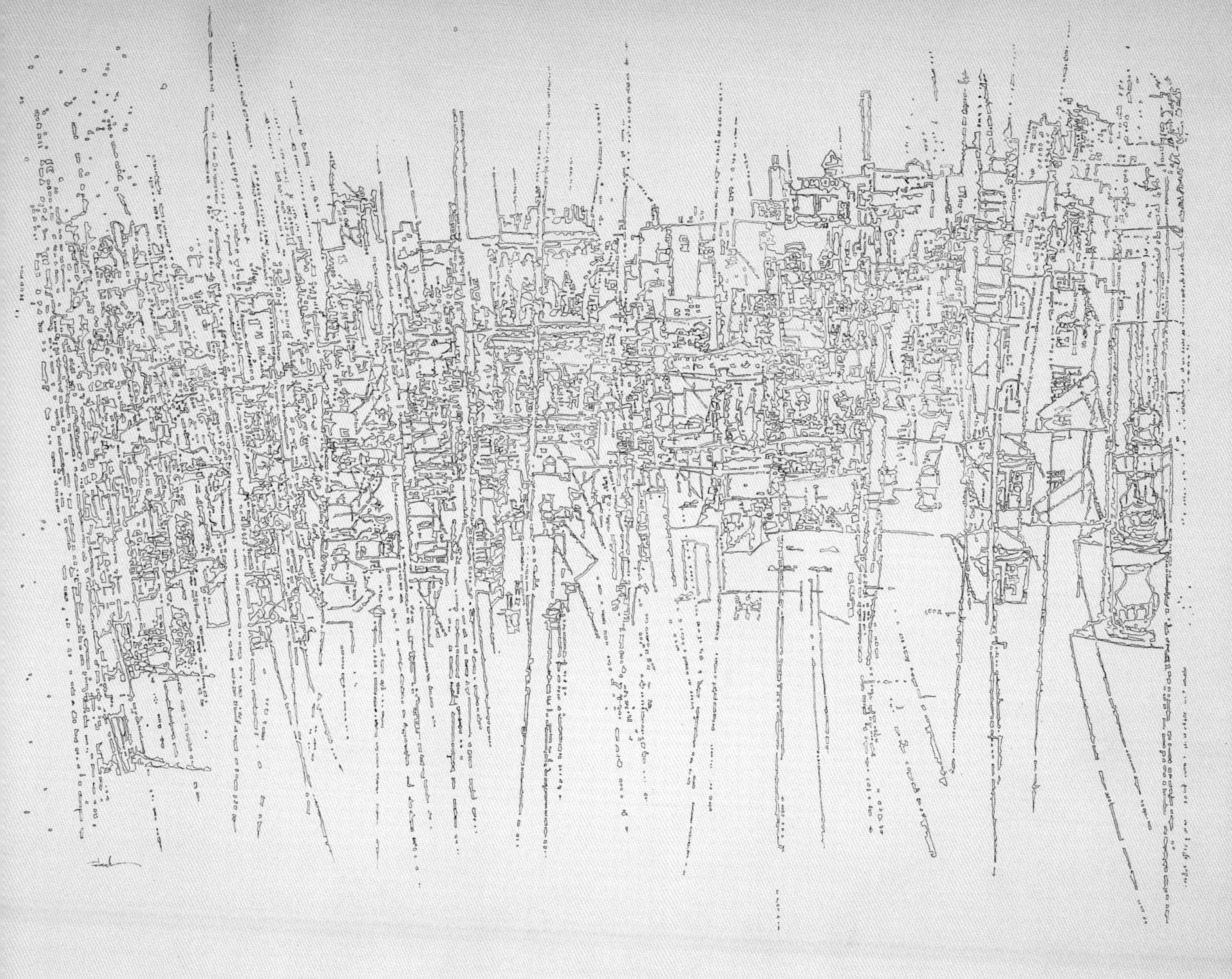

City
Geneva, 1984
pen and india ink on paper
22 1/2 x 30 1/8 inches

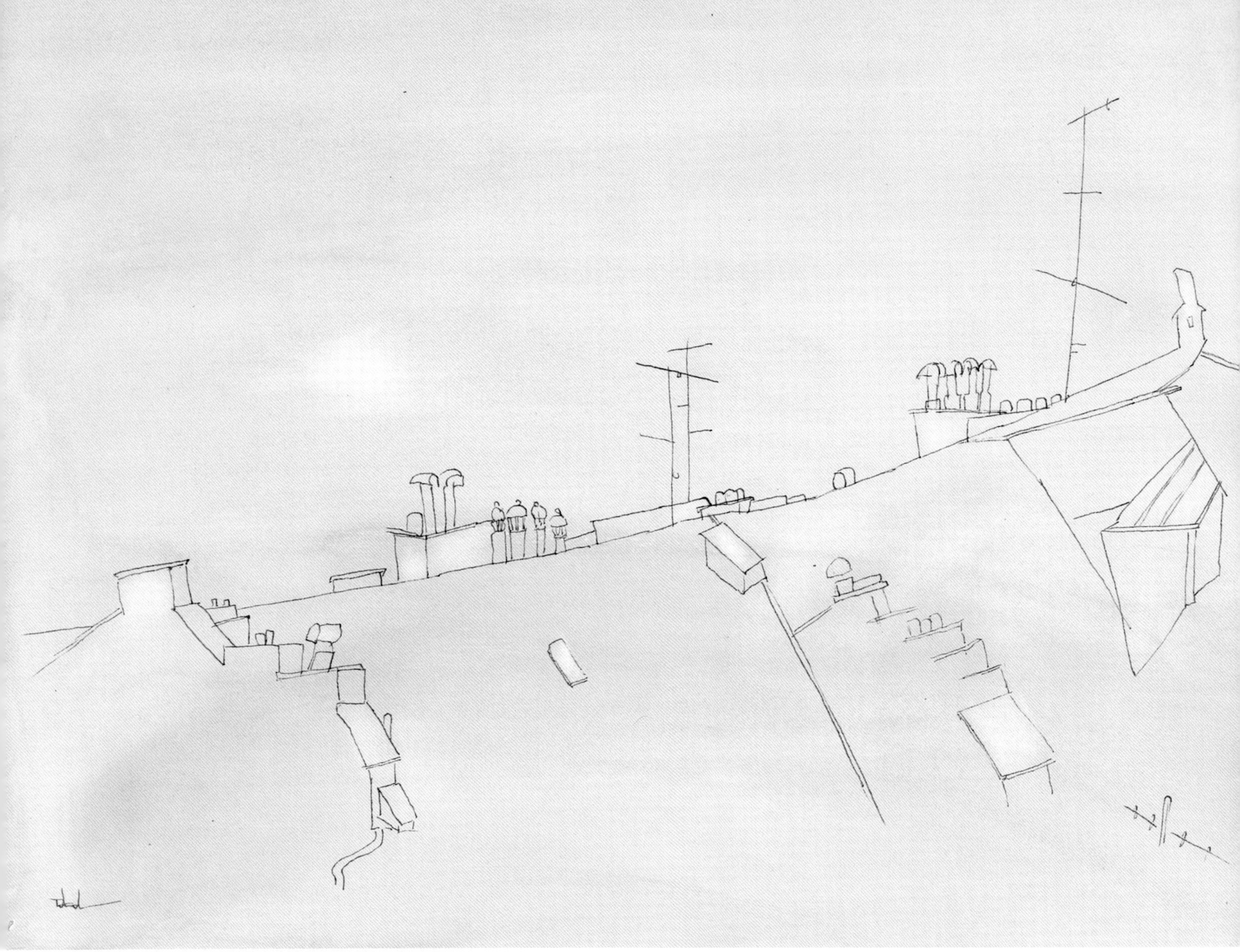

Chimney Pots and Antennas
Geneva, 1988
pen and india ink with brown wash on paper
9 1/4 x 11 7/8 inches

Face
Geneva, 1989
pen and india ink with red accents on paper
14 1/8 x 10 3/4 inches

Polluted City
Geneva, 1989
mixed media on paper
8 5/8 x 14 1/8 inches

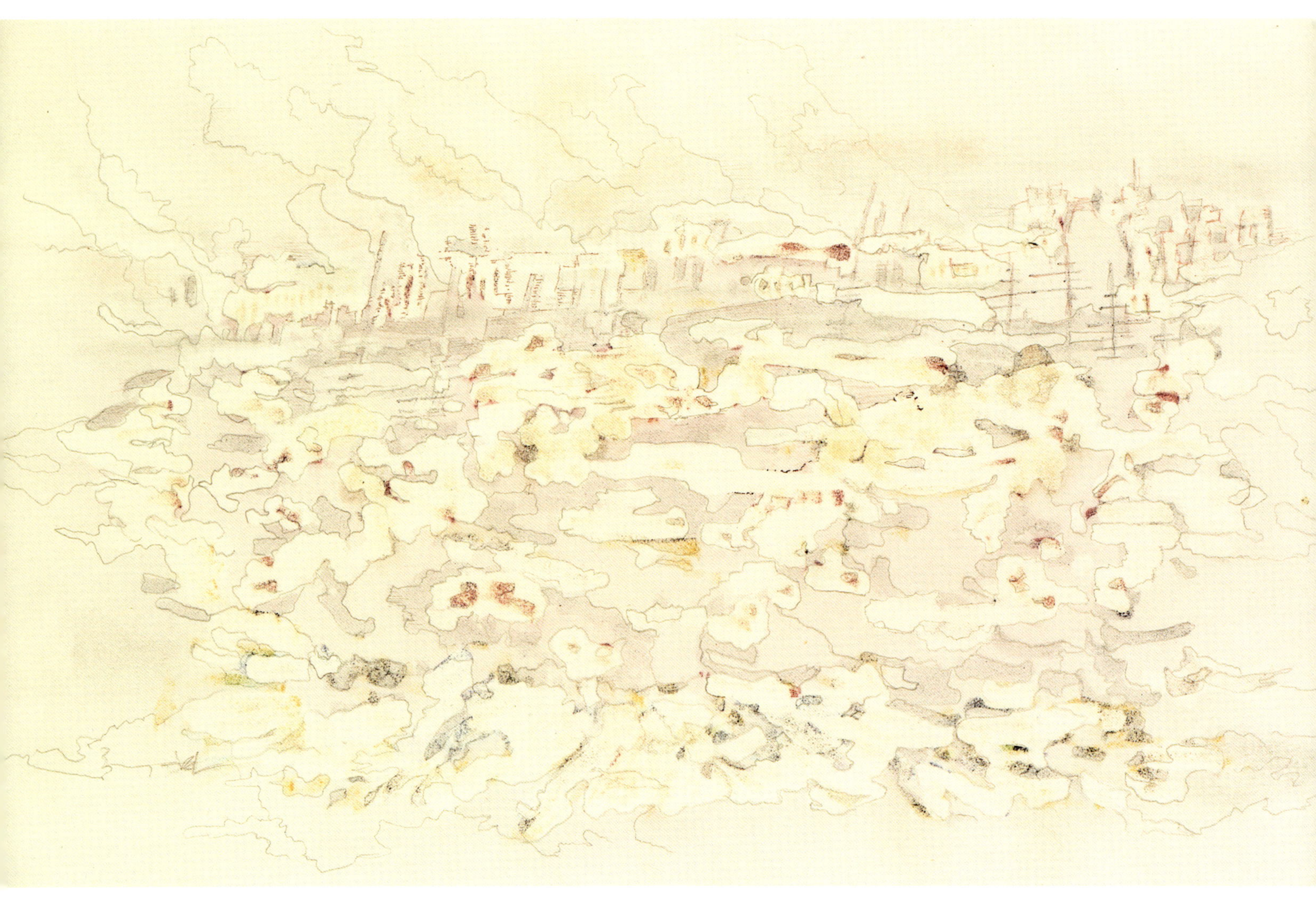

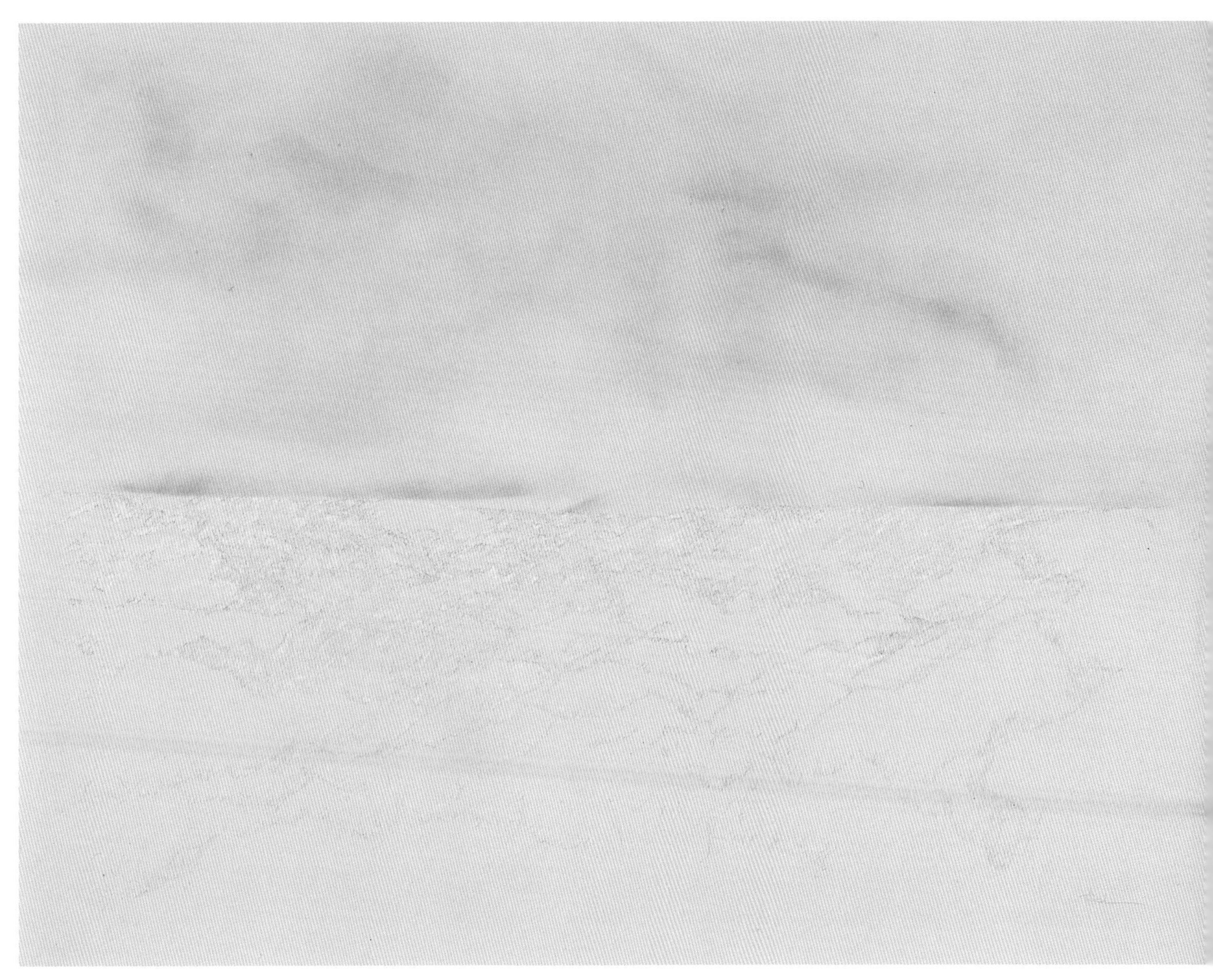

Field
Geneva, 1991
mixed media on gray-brown paper
20 x 26 1/8 inches

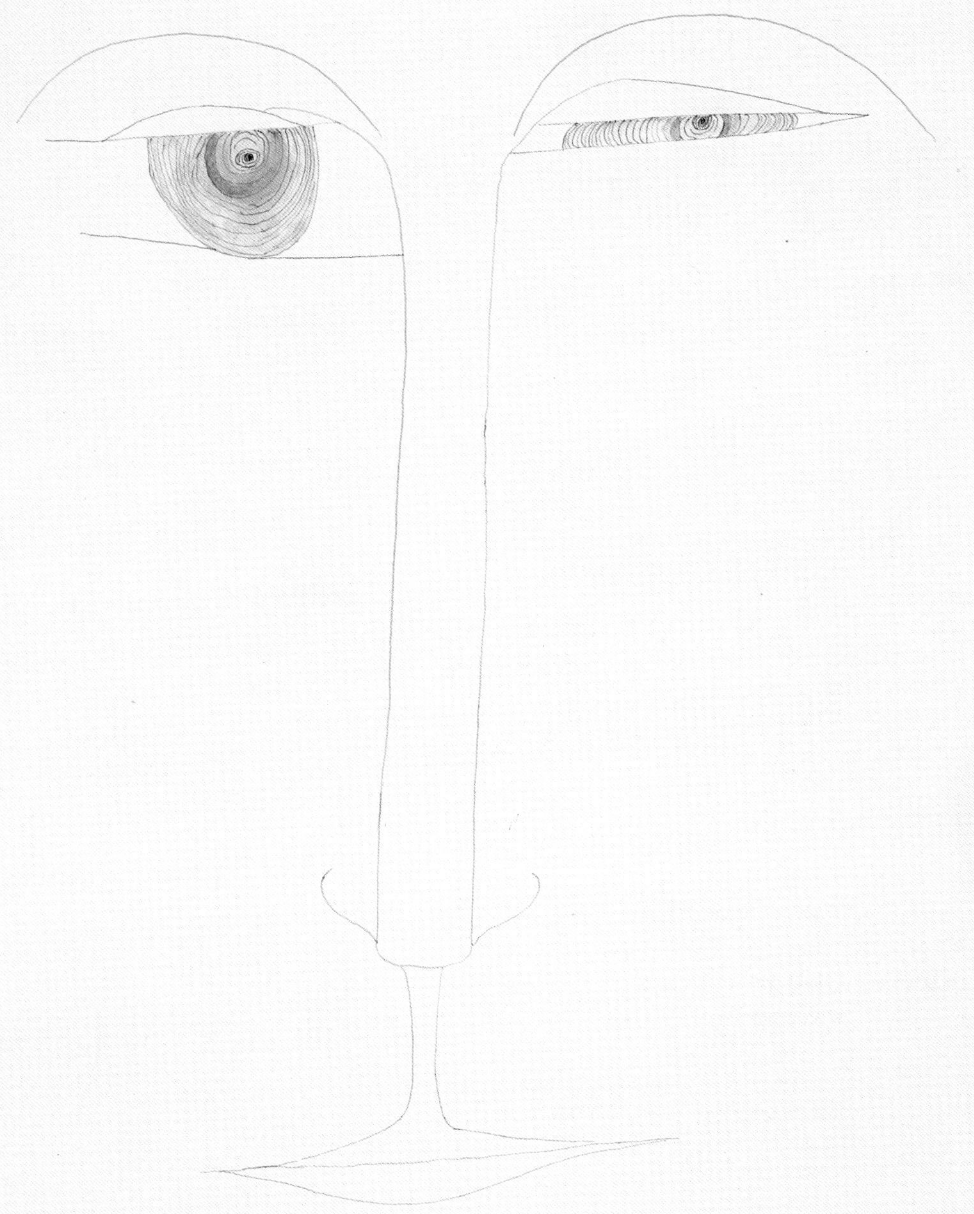

Face with Half-closed Eye
Geneva, 1992
pen and sepia ink with watercolor accents on paper
16 5/8 x 11 5/8 inches

92

Chronology

1905	Peter Takal, born in Bucharest, Romania
1910	Moves with his family to Berlin and Paris. Briefly attends life classes in Paris at the Académie Ranson, the Académie de la Grande Chaumière, and the Académie Colarossi
1920-38	Pursues stage and screen acting career in Germany and France
1932	First exhibition in Germany, Galerie Gurlitt, Berlin
1933	First exhibition in France, Galerie Zak, Paris
1935	University of Chicago professor Edward F. Rothschild sees Takal drawings at the Salon d'Automne, Paris, and presents them to Katherine Kuh Gallery in Chicago
1937	Travels to Casablanca, Morocco First exhibition in the United States, *Watercolors and Drawings by Picasso and Takal,* Kuh Gallery, Chicago
1939	Moves to New York
1941	First solo exhibition, Santa Barbara Museum of Art
1942	E.B. Crocker Art Gallery, Sacramento, and the M.H. de Young Memorial Museum, San Francisco, solo exhibitions
1944	Becomes an American citizen
1945	Acquires a farm in Saylorsburg, Pennsylvania, where he spends his summers and long holidays *Takal: Selected Works* published by International University Press, N.Y.
1956	Museum of Modern Art, New York, included in group exhibition, first of many
1957	Duveen-Graham Gallery, New York, circulates exhibition of Takal's drawings, prints and watercolors to 15 museums including the Arkansas Arts Center, the Los Angeles County Museum, the Minneapolis Institute of Arts, the University of Arkansas, Fayetteville, and the Dallas Museum of Art
1958	Solo exhibition, the Cleveland Museum of Art, ten additional venues through the Smithsonian Institution Traveling Exhibition Service
1960	Palazzo Strozzi, Florence, Italy, solo exhibition
1963-64	Tamarind Suite completed in Los Angeles—considered the pinnacle of his printmaking Everson Museum, Syracuse, solo exhibition
1967	Everhart Museum, Scranton, Pennsylvania, solo exhibition
1969	Moves to Geneva, Switzerland, and maintains a studio in Pennsylvania Carnegie-Mellon University, Pittsburgh, solo exhibition
1970	Galerie du Grand-Mézel, Geneva, forty-year retrospective
1986	Kresge Art Museum, Michigan State University, solo exhibition with catalogue raisonné
1992	*Danses,* a book of 32 reproductions of early drawings, published by Editions Weber, Geneva, Switzerland
1993	Pfalzgalerie, Kaiserslautern, Germany, solo exhibition, catalogue
1995	Died in Geneva
1998	Untitled (landscape), 1990, included in *Twentieth Century American Drawings from the Arkansas Arts Center Foundation Collection,* additional travel to ten venues, catalogue
2000	Arkansas Arts Center becomes the principal repository for the artist's work through a gift from the Takal Estate of over 2,000 drawings, plus prints and paintings

Select Public Collections

Canada	Montreal Museum of Art
Denmark	Royal Museum of Art, Copenhagen
England	Victoria and Albert Museum, London
France	Musée de l'Art Moderne de la Ville, Paris
	Bibliothèque Nationale, Cabinet des Estampes, Paris
Germany	Nationale Galerie, Berlin
	Staatsgalerie, Stuttgart
	Staatliches Kupferstichkabinett, Kassel
Italy	Gabinetto dei Disegni, Uffizi, Florence
Sweden	Nationalmuseum, Stockholm
Switzerland	Cabinet des Estampes, Geneva
United States	Achenbach Foundation for Graphic Arts, San Francisco
	Amon Carter Museum, Fort Worth
	Arkansas Arts Center, Little Rock
	Art Institute of Chicago
	Brooklyn Museum of Art
	Memphis Brooks Museum of Art, Tennessee
	Cincinnati Art Museum
	Cleveland Museum of Art
	Crocker Art Museum, Sacramento, California
	Dallas Museum of Fine Arts
	Indianapolis Museum of Art
	Joslyn Art Museum, Omaha, Nebraska
	Library of Congress
	Los Angeles County Museum of Art
	Metropolitan Museum of Art, New York
	M.H. de Young Memorial Museum, Fine Arts Museums of San Francisco
	Michigan State University, Kresge Art Museum, East Lansing
	Museum of Modern Art, New York
	National Gallery of Art, Washington, D.C.
	Pennsylvania Academy of the Fine Arts, Philadelphia
	Philadelphia Museum of Art
	St. Louis Art Museum
	Walker Art Center, Minneapolis
	Whitney Museum of American Art, New York
	Yale University Art Gallery, New Haven, Connecticut

Select Publications

John V. Brindle, *Graphics: Peter Takal,* Hunt Botanical Library, Carnegie-Mellon University, Pittsburgh, 1969.

Una E. Johnson et al, *Catalogue Raisonné of the Prints of Peter Takal,* Michigan State University, East Lansing, 1986.

Monique-Priscille Druey et al, *Takal: Dessins, 1930 - 1990,* Galerie Éditart D. Blanco, Gèneve, 1990.

Heinz Höfchen, *Peter Takal: Zeichnungen und Druckgraphik, 1930 - 1991,* Pfalzgalerie Kaiserslautern, Germany, 1993.

Gerald Nordland et al, *Twentieth Century American Drawings,* Arkansas Arts Center, Little Rock, 1998.